One Man's

One Man's Falklands . . .

Tam Dalyell

CECIL WOOLF · LONDON

First published 1 December 1982
Second impression before publication
Third impression 8 December 1982
©1982 Tam Dalyell

Cecil Woolf Publishers, 1 Mornington Place, London NW17RP
Tel: 01-387 2394

ISBN 0-900821-65-5 hardback edition
ISBN 0-900821-64-7 paperback edition

Contents

The Background from 1965

1965	UN General Assembly resolution calling for Anglo-Argentine talks about the Falklands.
1966	Armed commando of right-wing Peronist Argentines seize Port Stanley but eventually surrender.
Sept. 1967	Labour Foreign Secretary, George Brown, starts talks with Argentine Foreign Minister on the sovereignty of the islands. Britain prepared to forego sovereignty if assured that the islanders' rights and way of life can be preserved.
early 1968	Beginning of a campaign by a group of Conservative MPs to 'keep the islands British'.
Nov. 1968	Lord Chalfont fails to persuade the islanders of advantages of an agreement with Argentina.
Dec. 1968	Conservative spokesman on Foreign Affairs, Sir Alec Douglas Home, declares that if a Conservative government is returned it will 'strike sovereignty from the agenda'.
1970	Conservative government *is* returned under Edward Heath which *does* 'strike sovereignty from the agenda'.
1971	Argentina agrees temporarily to shelve their claim to sovereignty while they try to win the islanders over.
1973	Perónist government returns to power in Argentina and Argentine claims to sovereignty immediately renewed in UN.
late 1973	Governor of islands requests Royal Navy frigate to be sent, but is refused.
1977	Small group of Argentine sailors put ashore on British island of Morrell, South Sandwich Islands. Argentines claim this is for purposes of scientific research. British government, under James Callaghan, launches a new peace initiative, with question of sovereignty open to negotiation again.
Oct. 1977	Argentina starts preparing for naval 'manoeuvres', which alarm the British.
Nov. 1977	Callaghan sends two frigates and a nuclear submarine to the South Atlantic and Argentine naval 'activities' subside.
Nov. 1980	Conservative Minister of State (in Mrs Thatcher's government), Nicholas Ridley, suggests a 'lease-back' agreement to the islanders, which fails.
late 1981	Conservative government announce that HMS *Endurance* is to be withdrawn from the islands. British Antarctic Survey announce that budgetary cuts will mean closing their base at Grytviken on neighbouring island of South Georgia.

─────────────────────────────1982─────────────────────

2 Feb.   In a private letter to a Tory party activist the Prime
              Minister makes clear that she regards the presence of 75
              Royal Marines in Port Stanley as sufficient to prevent an
              Argentine invasion.
25 Feb.   Conservative Foreign Office Minister, Richard Luce, flies
              to New York for more talks with the Argentines, who
              suggest establishment of a negotiating commission, to
              meet monthly and to attempt to reach a conclusion by
              the end of 1982. (Argentina wants the islands back by
              1983, the 150th anniversary of British rule there.)
18 March   Scrap metal merchant, Constantine Davidoff, encouraged
              by Argentines to land illegally at Leith on British island
              of South Georgia with about 40 men.
26 March   SIS source in Buenos Aires warns that an Argentine
              invasion of Falklands is imminent, but government dis-
              misses warning. Argentine navy set out on scheduled
              manoeuvres with Uruguayan fleet.
28 March   Foreign Office minister, Richard Luce, begins to fear an
              invasion.
29 March   Joint Intelligence Committee reports to Britain that an
              invasion seems imminent.
2 April   Argentines arrive in Port Stanley and raise the Argentine
              flag.
              Emergency Cabinet meeting at 10 Downing Street.
Sat. 3 April House of Commons meets in an emergency session and is
              told that the task force is to be sent.
              Lord Carrington resigns.
              The Security Council of UN passes Resolution 502, order-
              ing cessation of all hostilities, withdrawal of all Argentine
              troops from the islands and calling upon Britain and
              Argentina to seek a diplomatic solution to their differences
              and fully to respect the purposes abd principles of the UN
              Charter.
7 April   Britain declares 200-mile war zone around Falklands.
9 April   American Secretary of State, Alexander Haig, undertakes
              mediation.
10 April   EEC, excluding Italy and Ireland, backs trade sanctions
              against Argentina.
17 April   Alexander Haig talks with Argentine military junta.
19 April   Haig negotiations break down.
              Peruvian initiative follows.
25 April   Royal Marines recapture South Georgia.
30 April   President Reagan publicly declares support for Britain.
2 May   Argentine cruiser *General Belgrano* sunk by British
              submarine outside war zone.
5 May   Peru drafts peace plan.
7 May   UN enter peace negotiations.

14 May	Prime Minister warns that peaceful settlement may not be possible.
17 May	Peace talks continue at UN as Mrs Thatcher speaks of 'one last go'.
19 May	UN peace initiative founders.
20 May	Mrs Thatcher accuses Argentina of 'obduracy and delay, deception and bad faith'. British task force ordered into battle.
21 May	British establish bridgehead at Port San Carlos, E. Falkland.
27 May	Darwin, Goose Green, Douglas and Teal inlet all taken by British.
4 June	Britain vetoes Panamanian-Spanish ceasefire resolution in UN Security Council.
15 June	Argentine garrison at Port Stanley surrenders, bringing cessation of fighting.
20 June	Britain re-takes South Sandwich Island.

Acknowledgements

I would like to record my real gratitude to the publishers, Cecil Woolf and Jean Moorcroft Wilson, who suggested a book outlining the view of a dissenter on the Falklands War, in the wake of their book, *Authors Take Sides on the Falklands*. In the preparation of *One Man's Falklands . . .*, I came to admire their scholarly and professional expertise, and their enthusiasm for the truth.

From their meeting of Sunday, 4 April and throughout the crisis I was given the deeply concerned support of West Lothian Constituency Labour Party Executive and General Management Committee. Many members challenged the opinions purveyed by newspapers, and raised the level of argument. I thank them. Their activity may explain why although I received a volume of critical and abusive mail from the south of England, I received only three critical letters from West Lothian, one of which was a good-natured poem parodying Robbie Burns.

Without the hard work in preparing the text of my wife Kathleen, this book would never have been completed. More fundamentally, I owe her, as usual, an intellectual debt, for her astute perceptions throughout the conflict, which she saw, earlier than I, as 'Mrs Thatcher's War'.

T.D.

1. *The Falklanders and their Friends*

It is easy to slide into a war. It is quite another matter to extricate oneself, even if that war was conceived as a short, sharp, simple police action. The Russians have found out this truth in Afghanistan and so have the British in Northern Ireland. Conflict gathers a momentum of its own. The original causes tend to recede into the distance. Protagonists are tempted to elevate their cause into high-sounding and totally irreconcilable principles. Thus in 1982 British ministers and ambassadors were trumpeting round the world that aggression must not be allowed to pay. Argentinian ministers and ambassadors were sounding off to the effect that there must be an end to colonialism in the Western hemisphere and that anachronistic ends of empire should not be tolerated. Whatever may have been superimposed afterwards in the way of argument, the immediate parliamentary reaction revolved around the fate of 1,800 islanders.

I must therefore dwell on the first of several sets of information stored in my mind, which caused my mental alarm bells to ring furiously on the 2nd and 3rd of April, 1982, when Britain heard of the Argentinian military aggression in the Falkland Islands. This was a profound scepticism of the case against closer relations with Argentina, vituperatively argued by certain articulate representatives of the Falkland islanders. At the same time I recognised that the real difficulty was that no Argentinian government had been willing to compromise on the issue of sovereignty; and that 'closer relations' could mean the beginning of the transfer of sovereignty.

After the return of the Labour Government in the first of the two 1974 general elections, I was chosen as the chairman of the Parliamentary Labour Party Foreign Affairs Group. Chairmen of back-bench groups receive all sorts of invitations: many involve jaunts; some involve serious work. One of the latter category was to attend a seminar at the Foreign Office on the problems of the Falkland Islands. I recollect wondering whether this was really a worthwhile use of my time, more of which might have been spent on the problems of Cyprus,

the Middle East, or a host of other seemingly more momentous
issues. However, at the request of the then Foreign Secretary,
James Callaghan, during one of our semi-regular Wednesday
evening meetings in his room in the House, I attended the
seminar and began to take an interest in what I thought at the
time to be a peripheral issue.

If I had pictured that the representatives of the Falklands
would be for the most part simple shepherds from the South
Atlantic, I could not have been more mistaken. On the
contrary, the case of the islanders was being put forward by
extremely competent, if long-winded, lawyers. Rightly or
wrongly, I had the distinct impression that, however eloquently
Foreign Office officials might try to sugar the pill, they would
never succeed in convincing the islanders of the benefits of
independence from Britain. The Falkland Islands Committee
were convinced that the Argentinians were trying to erode
British sovereignty or at least to bring about other compromises.
The Archangel Gabriel could not have talked Mr Hunter
Christie and his colleagues out of their deep suspicion of, and
antagonism towards, Argentina. They were intransigent.
Foreign Office men who wanted the representatives of the
Falkland islanders to be reasonable and accommodating
towards Argentina were near despair. There was no hope of a
meeting of minds. They were more British than the British.
Only among certain Ulster Protestants had I ever witnessed
this brand of exaggerated loyalty to Britain. Some of their
assumptions struck me as being those current in the mid-
nineteenth century. Added to this basic attitude, there was
the deep sense of grievance—some of it, I thought, justified—
that the British had not done more for the Falklanders.

My main contribution was to ask the representatives of the
Falkland islanders, gently if persistently, about their physical
dependence on Argentina. Victualling? Fuel supply? Medical
services? Education at later stages? Their response seemed to
be encapsulated in the assertion that if only we would provide
them with a decent airfield they would not be obliged to be
so dependent. They were clearly irritated and hurt when I
suggested that I could not believe airport facilities in Port
Stanley were a greater priority for the British taxpayer than
improvement of the then primitive facilities at Edinburgh
airport, which served thousands of times as many passengers.

They were clearly impatient of, and antagonistic to, any Labour MP, especially one who tactfully opined it was high time they came to terms with the twentieth century and took positive steps to develop a warmer relationship with Argentina in general and the Argentinians in South Patagonia in particular. After all, the South Patagonians lived in conditions very similar to their own rural, maritime surroundings.

I reported back to James Callaghan. To his credit, and doubtless as a result of a lot of other voices of no less weight than my own, the Foreign Secretary did the only thing he sensibly could and made a real attempt to find out the facts.

The Government set up a fact-finding Committee in 1976 and who better to lead it than Eddie Shackleton, former MP and Minister of Defence in the Lords and chairman of both the Parliamentary and Scientific Committee and Rio Tinto Zinc. He was also the son of the famous Arctic explorer, Sir Ernest Shackleton, who lay buried on South Georgia. The younger Shackleton's terms of reference were mainly economic. His mission was given the task of reporting on the islands' problems and potential. It would perhaps have been better if Shackleton had been commissioned to tackle the issue of the long-standing Argentine claim to sovereignty.

By the time he returned I was one of the members of the Labour delegation to the European Parliament and no longer at the centre of such issues as the Falklands, since I was no longer chairman of the PLP Foreign Affairs Group. The only thing that lodged firmly in my mind about the Shackleton Report was the bald fact of the magnitude of external land ownership — just under half the land (46%) and a quarter of the farms—the best farms. Much of the shouting about the obligations of the British to the Falklands and much of the reluctance to be wooed by Argentina, it dawned on me, had come from folk who spent more time in the United Kingdom than in the Falkland Islands. Indeed, during the important parliamentary debate on 14 April 1982, Michael McNair Wilson, MP for Newbury on Thames, was to put the case of 'one of my constituents and his family,' Mr John Matthews, who currently possessed 200,000 acres in the Falkland Islands.

The verbal clout of those Falkland islanders, who spend most of their time in Britain, has obscured a nagging question which to date has not been satisfactorily answered. How is it

that the Falkland islanders' perception of Argentina differs so
radically from that of the Scots and Welsh communities which
have kept their own heritage intact for many generations? In
1978, some of my constituents from West Lothian were able
to follow the Scottish team in their abortive quest for the
World Football Cup in Argentina. They were, they told me,
exceedingly well received by Mr Juan McCafferty and other
pillars of the Scots community in Argentina. The Welsh
communities in Argentina continue to speak Welsh and play
Rugby football, without fear or hindrance. For all the hard
politics of metropolitan Buenos Aires, why should the
Falklanders be treated so differently?

The notion put around that they would have to drive on
the right-hand side of the roads rather than the left smacks of
humbug. The discreditable truth is that outside Port Stanley,
the British have not coughed up the cash to make roads, and
those who have to manoeuvre Land Rovers over dirt tracks to
scattered sheep stations will pass each other according to the
nature of the terrain! Nor can it be deemed a great hardship
to require Falkland islanders to learn Spanish, if they have to
be treated in an emergency by Spanish-speaking doctors, or
send their offspring to Spanish-speaking schools. The
importance attached to the *English* way of life has been a
hypocrisy of a high order, given the realities of the position
of the Falklands.

One unspoken question was whether the interests of the
Falklanders and those of the United Kingdom necessarily
coincide; and, if not, on what criterion any perceived or real
differences should be assessed or resolved?

Nor at the beginning of April 1982 was I impressed by the
high-minded talk of the rights of small numbers of islanders.
If the rights of islanders were sacred, let alone submission by
Britain to the views or alleged views of islanders, why was it
that a British Government could so readily be a party to the
transportation of Diego Garcians from their own island in the
Indian Ocean to Mauritius? The Diego Garcians were dumped
on the quayside and told to make their own way as best they
could. In fact, they were to languish and lead miserable lives
in alien surroundings, simply because an Anglo-American
military base was required in the British Indian Ocean territories.
As one who had concerned himself deeply during the period

1966/70 with the fight to save Aldabra Atoll from Denis
Healey's conception of a staging post for the Royal Air Force,
and therefore with the related problems of the Chagos archi-
pelago, I could only marvel at the Labour Front Bench outrage
on behalf of the sanctity of islanders' rights. Mr Heath, Mr
Healey and others who were party to Diego Garcia, and any
politicians who ignored the protest of the Banabans, for
higher considerations of world politics, cannot swing round
in high moral dudgeon about the position of 1,800 mostly
white Falklanders. Yet it was these Falklanders who were
put on a pedestal by the British establishment and a large
part of the British media. The Falkland Islands Committee
had a crucial role in this process.

The Falkland Islands Committee is worth scrutiny. Night
after night, so it seemed throughout April 1982, we would
see the handsome profile of Air Commodore Frow appearing
on television on behalf of the Falklanders. When eventually
they attended a meeting in committee room 14 in the House
of Commons, on 27 April 1982, I asked the Air Commodore
if it was true that he had spent only a week in the Islands.
Much resentment was caused. It transpired that he had spent
three weeks in the Falklands. He was doing a highly professional
job.

After the same meeting I asked the wife of John Cheek, a
prominent member of the Falkland Islands Committee, about
what long term arrangements could be made to provide her
community with the necessities of life and medical requirements, if access to Argentina was no longer available.
Nobody has been able to provide a clear answer to this question.
As we shall see, no South American state is going to act as a
substitute for Argentina and therefore the unspoken answer
must be that Britain will have to develop an 8,000-mile
umbilical cord with the Falklands. My impression is that the
Falkland islanders had never thought through their long term
future before demanding British military help. Yet, ostensibly
at least, it was on their behalf that the British battle fleet
sailed to war, to the stark amazement of most of the world.

2. The Latin Americans

If experience of the Falklanders and their friends was the first element of my alarm at the beginning of April 1982, personal contact with South America, South Americans and Spaniards was the second. Few MPs of the present Parliament have had my good fortune in going to the continent. For MPs travel to Europe, West and East can be frequent, under a variety of auspices of British and EEC origin. The Commonwealth Parliamentary Association makes possible many visits to countries of the Commonwealth. The British American Parliamentary Group and many foundations make possible travel to the United States and Canada. Chances of visiting the Latin American world, however, are few. In 1975 I had led the Inter-Parliamentary Union Delegation to Brazil; but since most South American Parliaments (in so far as institutions recognisable as Parliaments exist), are at the embryo stage, contacts have been difficult. A few MPs, such as Norman Buchan, on ministerial agricultural business, and Cecil Parkinson, ironically destined to be a member of the War Cabinet, on trade business, and Neville Trotter, from Tyneside, have actually set foot in Buenos Aires. However, whereas the House of Commons is collectively well informed about the Middle East, and rather well informed about the Far East and the rest of the world, there was a collective ignorance about South America and the Hispanic world when the conflict arose. It would hardly be an exaggeration to suggest that it seemed to many British MPs that they were dealing simply with ignorant, cruel, 'fascist dagos'; and such was the stirring of the emotions by the British newspapers, not all of them tabloids, that it was difficult to persuade them otherwise.

From the day that I first set foot on South American soil at São Paulo Airport, and was taken immediately to the Aerospace Centre at San Jose dos Campos to see the satellite education programme and an aircraft factory, I was struck by the sophistication of their industry. As an MP whose main interest is in science and technology, I recognised at once the high quality of much of the work being done and the obvious ability of those in charge, both at a managerial and a technical level. Clearly I betrayed my surprise, which prompted my hosts to point firmly to achievements, not only in Brazil but in Argentina and other South American countries. Far from being the classic developing country, I was told that Argentina derived 37% of her gross national product from industry, the same percentage as the Federal Republic of Germany. It is preposterous to think of the great nations of South America as backward. Any nation that has the capability of marrying an Exocet missile to the wing of an aircraft, as Argentina did before sinking HMS *Sheffield*, must have some brilliant engineers in computer and fusing technology, even though they almost certainly received help from the French.

From the first day of this visit, all seemed sweetness and light between Brazilians and British, other than on one, to me, rather unexpected topic — the Malvinas. Time and again, either in response to the question, 'Are there any difficulties between us?' — or unprompted — complaint was politely registered on the colonial situation in the Falkland Islands. The bother and unease spread right across the political spectrum. An Anglophile right-winger, Senator Herbert Levy of São Paulo, said gently but firmly that British rule in the Falklands was a festering sore, about which 'you will have to do something'. This came from a friend of Britain who had no particular love of Argentina and was less than enamoured of the performance of successive Argentinian governments. From the centre of Brazilian public life, from men like Senator Broges of the Arena Party, and the Cambridge-educated doctor who was Governor of Recife, the same warnings came. They contended that there were two separate but intertwined issues — decolonisation and the succession to Spanish sovereignty; that Argentina succeeded to Spanish sovereignty over the Falklands; that the establishment of a British settlement there was and remained illegal; and that the maintenance of British rule over the settlement, illegal from the outset, had become anachronistic. From the Left, the opposition MDB Party, there was an insistence that British hegemony over the Falkland Islands was an insult to Latin America as a whole, not simply to Argentina. How does a Socialist justify, I was pointedly asked, British rule over a place more than 8,000 miles from London and 400 miles from

the South American mainland? I was left in no possible
doubt that even among those who had no time for right-wing
governments, disliked military dictatorships and in some cases
had themselves personally suffered at the hands of the
military, there was growing impatience with the British
position on the Falklands/Malvinas. However, only once,
according to my notes of seven years ago, was I explicitly
warned that there could one day be armed combat over the
Malvinas. Significantly enough, the warning came from
Admiral Faria Lima, Governor of Rio de Janeiro and a former
head of Petrobras, the Brazilian National Oil Corporation,
who could be assumed to have had contacts with the Argentinian rulers in various capacities.

What was obvious was that Right, Centre and Left, whatever
their other differences, and whatever their attitude towards
their southern neighbour, Brazilians were at one in the belief
that Britain should cede sovereignty of the Falkland Islands
to Argentina. Such sentiments emanated not only from those
of Iberian Portuguese/Spanish descent, but also from those
Southern German-speaking Brazilians from Santa Catherina
Province and Rio Grande del Sul, who tended to be critical
of Argentinian leaders on other grounds.

It was also the experience of this visit to Brazil that was to
distance me from many of my friends in the Parliamentary
Labour Party, such as Stanley Clinton Davies and Stanley
Newens, who had a history of energetic campaigning on issues
of human rights in South America. (As I shall seek later to
argue, it was their influence that endowed the launching of
the task force with a respectability in the Labour movement
which it would not otherwise have enjoyed.) Sensitive to the
opinion of several members of the PLP Foreign Affairs Group,
of which I was chairman, that I should not be going to Brazil,
and allow myself to be 'used', I was extremely careful to see
as many people as possible in Brazil concerned with questions
of human rights. Among those with impeccable credentials
of concern for human freedoms was Dom Ivo Lorschreider,
then Secretary of the Bishops' Conference, now a Cardinal
Archbishop. He quietly observed to the British delegation
that, though there had been terrible excesses in parts of South
America, those who had responsibility for Northern Ireland
might do well to consider the mote in their own eye. Law

and order in areas of South America, where half the population was under 19 years of age was not a simple matter of right and wrong, black and white. It was all very well for Europeans, coming from stable societies to wax eloquent about human rights, but if we British had to use force in Northern Ireland, we should be careful about condemning those in burgeoning cities like São Paulo and Buenos Aires, for denying human rights. Confronted by Dom Ivo's plea to restrain rash judgements about human rights, I recollected the dinner a few nights before, when as leader of the British delegation, I had sat next to our host, Egidio Martins, then Governor of São Paulo, who poured out his heart on the impossibilities of running an expanding megalopolis. How would *I* keep law and order in a city of 16 million? São Paulo, Mexico City and Buenos Aires presented problems *sui generis* which had only been solved in Mao's China, where they had refused to allow even close relatives of citizens of Shanghai to join their families, because it would have added an unbearable strain on a city of ten million. Only ruthless state action, possible in Mao's China but impossible in Latin America, could really cope with the problem. The following day, Dr Setubal, director of transport for São Paulo asked me how I would like providing sewers, schools, transport and other amenities, for a city that was expanding at the rate of the entire population of my native Edinburgh every year, each year in the decade. Substitute, I thought in April 1982, Buenos Aires for São Paulo, and you have a problem in which human rights may not be seen in black and white terms.

Since I may seem to be leading up to something of an *apologia* for the behaviour of successive Argentinian governments towards the human rights of their own citizens, I must content myself with observing that human rights in Argentina is basically a metropolitan Buenos Aires problem and that it ill behoves politicians in Britain, who would be hard put to it to run the proverbial whelk-stall, to conclude that the battle fleet should be despatched to the South Atlantic for fear that the human rights of the rural Falklanders should be affected by the furnace of the Buenos Aires megalopolis. The problem of lack of respect for human rights is manifestly much more acute in big cities than in rural areas, where other problems take first place; and the Falklands are rural.

Those who saw the despatch of the task force in terms of some great crusade mounted against Argentinian tyrants of their own people have to explain the awkward fact that those who had been persecuted were united with their persecutors on one issue, if only one issue—the retaking of the Malvinas. European champions of the cause of Latin American human rights who suggested, as Michael Foot did on 7 April 1982, at the PLP meeting that British action would help those who were struggling for freedom in Argentina, have to explain the behaviour of those who had themselves suffered most from the oppressive Junta. Peres Esquivel, the Nobel Prize winner, came to Europe to plead for understanding on the Malvinas: no man, enduring personal hardship, had more reason to loathe his current Government. Sections of the Montanneros, political heirs of Evita Perón who have been conducting a running fight on the streets of Buenos Aires with the forces of the military Junta, were to declare themselves shoulder to shoulder with their domestic foes on this issue. The truth is that whereas some British authorities and a section of the British public feel that Britain has a right to the Islands, 8,000 miles distant, to all Argentinians the Malvinas is an integral part of their country.

The vehemence of this feeling was brought home to me when, as a member of the European Parliamentary Latin America Committee, I attended two ten-day delegate conferences, one in Mexico City and another in Strasbourg. Talking late into the night, sometimes with men from the other side of the continent—Colombia, Ecuador and Peru— it was clear that they could not have a serious talk with a British MP without at least a passing reference to the Malvinas. I also learned another incontrovertible fact in my time as a member of the European Parliament, which weighed heavily with me, years later, throughout April 1982: the Italians, the Germans and the French, in that order, had an infinitely more serious conception of their cultural and trading relations with South America than we the British had. Our Consul-General in São Paulo, the late Sir George Hall, who tragically died in post as Ambassador in Brasilia, used to complain sadly that great British companies, with a few distinguished exceptions, found it impossible to make sustained efforts in the Latin American market. His view was amply confirmed

both by the politicians and by the industrialists who came to
the Strasbourg Parliament. From the beginning of April I was
convinced that talk of sanctions by our EEC partners might
last for a little while but would soon wither away. It was a
non-starter in the mind of anyone who knew Europeans and
their relations with South America to suppose that the
imposition of sanctions was any more than window-dressing
and short-term posturing. European governments could never
have intended sanctions against Argentina to bite. Predictably,
the Italians and the Irish excused themselves from the
imposition of sanctions at the earliest decent opportunity. In
West Germany, Siemens made it clear to their Government
that they were averse to having their many contracts in
Argentina and South America disrupted or desynchronised,
simply because of Britain's 'mad war' (Chancellor Helmut
Schmidt's words) in the Falklands. French industry, whatever
the formal statements from the Quai d'Orsay, went merrily
on its way, selling where it could in South America and even,
as we now suspect, helping the Argentinians with the Exocets
it had already sold them. Besides, the use of sanctions was
bound to be futile, when every one of her neighbours was
more or less sympathetic to the Argentinian cause and all
that sanctions-busters had to do was to send their goods via
Montevideo or Rio de Janeiro. As we shall see, it was
quickly discovered that, since the Argentinian debt to the
West was some four times that of Poland's, the lender, in the
person of Western banks, might well be harder hit than the
borrowers, in the financial institutions of Argentina. What I
learned in the European Parliament was that, just as there are
many members of the House of Commons who value their
relations with English-speaking North Americans in the United
States and Canada, so equally there are many members of
the Chamber of Deputies in Rome, the Bundestag and the
Assemblé Nationale who value their friends in South America,
many of whom are at home in Italian, French or German. It
should not be forgotten that in the days after the sinking of
the *General Belgrano*, lists of local names appeared in the
newspapers of Palermo, Bari and Naples.

It was clear to me from the word go that after the initial
shock at the prospect of actual shooting over the Falkland
Islands, the European reaction to the task force would range

from wide-eyed incredulity at the British reaction to contempt and scorn for the shedding of blood and loss of life. The *Frankfurter Allgemeine* and the *Sud-Deutscher Zeitung* both regretted that the Falklands had renewed the respectability of bloodletting by a European state. Whatever the official etiquette adopted by governments, any British traveller in Europe knows that this is indeed the case.

I have received much abuse for my attempt to put the South American viewpoint and so, too, has Judith Hart. Yet of all Labour MPs none has taken a more sustained long-term interest in the problems of Latin America than we have — I on the trade side and Judith on the human rights side. Naturally we have a number of friends in common and among them is Christopher Roper, of *Latin American Newsletter*, who was a member of the Labour Party Latin American Study Group set up by the National Executive Committee. Throughout the crisis I talked almost daily to him, as a Labour Party colleague. I have his permission to publish part of his eloquent letter of 19 April 1982 to Michael Foot, Denis Healey and John Silkin:

> It seems that few people in either the Labour or the Conservative Parties understand why Latin American opinion, Left, Centre and Right, is overwhelmingly in favour of Argentina's claim to the Falkland Islands. This is not a question of human rights, but of territorial rights, and most Latin Americans see the occupation of the islands as a piece of unfinished business in the long struggle to liberate Latin America from European domination.
>
> It is simply not true to say that dissident groups in Argentina hope the British will succeed in order to bring down the government of Galtieri. The opposition will continue to oppose Galtieri on a whole range of issues, including the fate of the disappeared, political prisoners, freedom of association in political parties and trade unions, economic policy, education and health policies, and so on. But they will support the only government they have in this confrontation with Britain.
>
> I do not think it will do to say that the Falkland Islanders wish to remain British and should therefore so remain. But for an historical accident, their situation would be no

different from that of millions of other emigrants who left the old world for the new, acquiring a new nationality on the way. You perhaps noticed the slogan in Comodoro Rivadavia (it appeared on television) saying Argentinians and Welsh together will throw out the English.

It seems to me quite significant that two of the MPs who have shown most active concern for the affairs of Latin America, Judith Hart and Tam Dalyell, should both be speaking firmly against the task force, not merely on grounds of expediency, but of principle.

If, as Tam Dalyell has claimed, the joint chiefs of staff really advised against the sending of the task force, what in heaven's name are we doing supporting it?

I wrote a letter to *The Times* last week (unpublished) in which I argued strongly against any attempt to retake the islands by force (and force must be intended if the threat of force is to have any credibility) on the grounds:

a. That it would finally destroy the fragile social economy of the island community;
b. Would recreate the fading image of Britain as a piratical colonial power; and
c. That even if we were victorious the islands would remain in practice (if not name) dependencies of Argentina.

Our present policy, comprehensible in the mouths of Tory backwoodsmen, betrays an alarming ignorance of Latin American realities. The real failure was not the Foreign Office's, but of successive governments, which well knew that we had neither the will nor the means to retain the Falkland Islands as an integral part of the United Kingdom, but never dared explain this unpalatable fact to the inhabitants of the Falkland Islands and to the people of this country.

Nor was it simply those who could be vilified as European do-gooders who tried to see the other side of the picture. I have permission to publish two other letters written to the Leader of the Labour Party — one from the Argentine Refugee Group in London and the other from John Gannon, one of the hard-headed leaders of the Association of Scientific, Technical and

Managerial Staffs, who has personal experience of Argentina. Both these letters repeat Roper's point that Latin American opinion would be solidly behind Argentina, if only on this issue (see Appendix E).

The generality of politicians can be forgiven for not knowing much about South America before 1 April 1982. What is less forgivable is, that whether or not they felt able to influence events, few politicians bothered to find out about the background to the current crisis. Indeed, when the University of Stirling invited all 71 Scottish MPs on 24 April to a one-day seminar, over which they had taken considerable trouble, with a number of distinguished speakers,* I was the only MP to turn up. The fact is that the modern MP tends to be inundated with day-to-day affairs in his constituency and we are all at fault in not giving our whole minds to the central issues which face the state. At Stirling, and from Peter Flynn of the Department of Latin American Studies in Glasgow University, I learned certain aspects of Argentine history of which I was either unaware or only dimly aware. Some seemed pertinent to the present day.

The first thing I learnt was that Argentina, part of the Spanish Vice-Royalty of La Plata, was an unattractive colony for the early Spaniards because it lacked the gold and silver of Mexico and Peru. However, in the view of every school textbook, the Vice-Royalty included the Malvinas/Falkland Islands.

I also learnt that Britain's role in Argentine history was considered important. For in 1806 Sir Hugh Popham sailed without instructions from Southern Africa to attack Buenos Aires. For this the Government proposed to court martial him, but was restrained from doing so by public opinion and had to accept the *fait accompli*. Indirectly this helped the inhabitants overthrow the Vice-Royalty of La Plata and led to the foundation of an independent Argentina on 25 May

---

*Professor D.A.G. Waddell of Stirling; R.G. Storey, a member of the Highlands and Islands Development Board who was a member of Lord Shackleton's team which prepared the report on the Falkland Islands in 1976; Professor R.W. Medhurst, of the Department of Political Studies and an expert on Juan Perón and the legacy of Perónismo; Philip O'Brien of the Institute of Latin American Studies at Glasgow University; and Mr G.A. Makin, an Argentinian from Cambridge.

1810. Modern Argentinians could not at first believe that
their aircraft carrier, the *Veintecino de Mayo*, might have
been used against those who had helped their assertion of
independence in 1810, even though Britain had walked the
tightrope of neutrality in order not to antagonise the
Spaniards too much since we were currently in the throes of
the Peninsula War with France. The service Britain performed
was to refuse to allow any other European power to interfere.

Later in the 19th century, it appeared, Argentina was one
of those cases of 'informal empire' in which Britain dominated
the economy. The British Government was careful not to
become involved. Argentina was consumed by internal
divisions, immigrants versus established residents (many of
whom were Anglo-Saxon), cattlemen versus townsmen. The
Anglo-Argentine community had always been well treated
and, at first in 1982, they simply could not believe that the
British would move against them. When it became apparent
that Mrs Thatcher was in earnest, however, quite a number of
the sons of the Anglo-Argentine community volunteered to
join the armed forces—the Argentine not the British forces.
A young man living in Buenos Aires, son of a well known
Anglo-Argentine, who had shared a tank with Francis Pym
during World War II, was no exception in wanting to join the
Argentine forces, so strongly did they feel over the Malvinas.

Apart from the running sore over the Falkland Islands, which
Argentine claimed as part of the inheritance from Spain, as a
result of successful revolution, the only disagreement
concerned tariff reductions and Imperial Preference during
the depression of the 1930s. The Rocker-Runciman Agreement of 1933 created great resentment, as it allowed beef
into the British market at a reduced tariff but at a disadvantage
to Imperial Preference. During World War II, though British
manufactured goods were no longer available and foreign
assets were liquidated, many Argentinians helped the British
war effort. After the war, an approach was made to the Attlee
Government over the Malvinas, on the basis, common to
South American law, that territorial jurisdiction depended on
the ownership of land and not on occupation by groups of
people from an albeit homogenous British background. This
claim was supported among others by the groups of Scots
settlers, brought together in the St Andrew's Society of the

River Plate, the Welsh Patagonians who had retained their cultural identity since the 19th century, and by successive editors of *The Buenos Aires Herald*, including James Neilson.

Moreover, as I was to explain at two meetings of the PLP, the standard work on the subject, published in 1927 by an American academic with the unfortunate name of Jules Goebel, came down, after 460 pages of history and turgid law, firmly on the side of the Argentinian claim. It had puzzled me for years that the British, who profess themselves to be great believers in the International Court of Justice, had been so coy about referring the Falklands/Malvinas argument to the Hague: now I began to understand. Successive British governments and their advisers had not been sufficiently confident that they would win their case and Goebel's *The Struggle for the Falklands* indicated why not.

Goebel points out that the fundamental principle of territorial arrangements in South America is the *Uti Possidetis* of 1810. By this principle is understood the claim of the several republics carved out of the Spanish colonial empire to the regions embraced in the former Spanish administrative units. So the limits of the Buenos Aires vice-royalty were taken as those of the Argentine Confederation. Goebel had no doubt that the Falklands formed part of this vice-royalty: the mere fact that they were ultimately placed under the same governorship as the South Patagonian settlements was sufficient proof. The principle of *Uti Possidetis* would sustain the claim of sovereignty as against all other South American states. For Goebel, it was immaterial as to whether or not it would sustain a claim against Great Britain; for, in relation to the Falklands, the Argentine claim was supported by the practice of nations in matters that have been generally called questions of 'state succession'. Where a new state is formed of a pre-existing body politic, either by succession or by union of formerly sovereign states, the new state succeeds to the rights and obligations of the mother state. So Goebel concludes that the British notion that the Argentine Confederation could not have an interest in a cause settled between England and Spain is totally without legal foundation. Goebel asserts the right of the Argentinian nation to stand in the place of Spain with regard to the sovereignty over the Falklands: it was established by successful revolution and by the assertion

and maintenance of sovereignty over the Falklands as against
Spain. When Great Britain seized the islands in 1833, the
legal consequences were the same as if the islands had never
passed out of the hands of the Spanish crown. Goebel believed
that the British had 'suborned' the law to cover imperialistic
designs.

Having read Goebel for myself I came to the conclusion
that Argentina's claims were far stronger than had been
represented in Britain. However, when I tried to interest the
press in my discoveries, only *The Times'* 'Diary' responded.
From that brief mention arose a contact which was to
confirm my doubts as to Britain's claim. It came from Dr
Peter Beck, an historian and international relations specialist,
who had been researching into the Falklands dispute for
several years. In a letter of 28 May 1981, Dr Beck informs
me of the withdrawal 'for research' by the Foreign Office of
most of the files relating to the dispute over sovereignty of
the Falklands since 1910. (These files were originally at the
Public Record Office and therefore available to the public.)
Dr Beck had himself written a study indicating the
uncertainty in the Foreign Office from 1910 onwards, which
had been bought by *The Sunday Times*, but not published
by them until after the British had retaken the Falklands —
for patriotic reasons, the editor maintained. (See Appendix
B for Dr Beck's letter in full, pp. 135-36). It finally appeared
on 20 June 1982 in the 'Insight' column under the title
'Sovereignty: the Secret Doubts'. Had it appeared earlier, as
the young *Sunday Times* journalist Christopher Hird had
wished, it might well have altered events.

Once Dr Beck's work was in the open, I could write to
Francis Pym on 22 June asking more specific questions than
my previous rather generalised ones about the legality of our
claims. The Foreign Secretary replied personally to my four
main questions, but dismissed 'the comments made in the
past at various dates by individual officials in the FCO' as 'a
few isolated and selective expressions of doubt' (for the
author's letter to Francis Pym and Mr Pym's reply, see
Appendix B, pp. 136-38). In commenting on Pym's reply,
The Sunday Times' 'Insight' columnist maintained that he
had 'examined many files at the Public Record Office, from
both the Foreign Office and the old Colonial Office. These

show that, until the beginning of the Second World War, British government actions were shaped by doubts over our claim to the islands, and that these doubts were not the isolated opinions of a few individuals'. The doubts arose from those experts like Gaston de Bernhardt, who were in the Foreign Office precisely to perform that kind of role.

There is only one possible deduction to be drawn from the British government's wish to eschew going to court and taking the legal road. The ministers most closely involved in the Falklands 'loss' had come to believe that only a successful military and naval action could retrieve their reputations. Thus the British strategy had to be short-term strategy, where the delay involved in legal proceedings could not be brooked. Haste was essential if political careers were to be rescued. The excuse was ready to hand: if we did not move fast, Argentine forces would be more difficult to winkle out of the Falklands. I do not doubt that, later in the negotiations, ministers came to believe quite genuinely that the Junta was playing for time: but in early April, as President Galtieri told Oriana Fallaci, in her celebrated interview published in *The Times* of 12 June 1982, he and his colleagues were genuinely amazed at the British reaction.

The counter question can properly be asked. Why did not Argentina go to the Courts at the Hague? The Brazilian ambassador, Roberto Campos, explained to me that South Americans saw the International Court as a European/United States/Developed World institution, in which Latin Americans could have little confidence. He did not suggest that they were correct in this perception, but gave it as an explanation for Argentina's failure to submit their case to the Courts.

There was one other point concerning South America which lent itself to so much scoffing among MPs, that I soon refrained from making it for fear of damaging the case. None the less, I believe it to be an important truth. Europeans are appalled by minor military aggressions and coups. In South America, if they are not regarded as routine, at least they have a familiar look. I have the impression that few people in Argentina, and not very many in Latin America, comprehended the enormity of what they had done when they sent troops to the Falklands. The reaction tended to be, 'Well, we did it without spilling a drop of British blood, even though we lost some of our own occupying forces, but we meant to make that sacrifice!' Such considerations do not excuse the action; they do, however, help to explain why Argentinians could not believe their eyes and ears which told them the task force was on its way.

Personal experience of Latin America served to shield me against a brace of other canards that were being floated around at the beginning of April 1982: 'If we do not resist in the Falklands it will be an open invitation to Venezuela to attack Guyana, to settle their differences of opinion on their common border and it will provide an all-clear signal for Guatamala to invade Belize.'

Now it so happens that my brother-in-law, Father Anthony Wheatley, is a Jesuit priest who has worked in Guyana and other parts of Latin America. He points out that as a leading member of the Organisation of American States, Venezuela is hardly likely to incur the wrath of the continent by launching an invasion of some of the most difficult jungle country on the face of the planet. Moreover, decisions in Caracas on Venezuelan claims to the upper areas of the Essequibo River are unlikely to be affected by considerations of whether a European power decides to intrude in a military capacity in the Western hemisphere. Caracas will be guided by the interplay of intra-hemispheric relations and its perceptions of the Venezuelan national interest and not by self-styled high-mindedness in London. Furthermore, is it really suggested that in the remote event of a Venezuelan attack on Guyana, we sent the British fleet to Georgetown or Caracas, to conduct war on behalf of the Government of Guyana which has one of the worst human rights records against the Government of Venezuela, a democracy which has one of the best records on human rights? Such a notion should be dismissed as moonshine, in the same category of daftness as the idea that we had to go to the Falklands to show that we really meant to defend Hong Kong. Ten seconds reflection brought those MPs who articulated the need to defend 'Hong Kong in the South Atlantic', to wince at the thought of taking on one thousand million Chinese in a military capacity, for the sake of our Hong Kong lease.

Belize I know a good deal about at first hand, having stayed in Balmapan, as the guest of the Governor, Mr Peter

McEntee, and also with the Colonel commanding the Irish
Guards, outside Belize City. Belize is different from the
Falklands in many respects but in one above all others.
Whatever they may have thought about the Argentinian
military action in the first place, no one in South America
disputes the Argentinian claim to the Malvinas; most of South
America strongly disputes Guatamala's claim to Belize, and
in particular and crucially, Mexico would not countenance a
Guatamalan take-over. The Mexicans are content to see an
independent Belize and have no desire to take on the problems
of a run-down colony for which Britain has done far too
little. However, if anyone, say the Mexicans to George Price,
the Belize Prime Minister, is to annexe Belize, it should be
the descendants of the Maya Empire. As visitors to the superb
Museum of Anthropology in Mexico City will see, the Maya
Empire extended into what was to become British Honduras.
In Spanish times more of Belize belonged to the Captaincy-
General of Yuccatan than to the Captaincy-General of
Guatamala. The links of Belize are more with the Yuccatan
civilisation in Mexico than with Guatamala City and therefore
Mexico is our friend.

These were the amalgam of experiences and considerations
which prompted my interruption of the Prime Minister on
that historic morning of Saturday, 3 April, during her opening
speech: 'The Right Hon. Lady referred to our many friends.
Have we any friends in South America on this issue?'

3. The Military

To a greater or lesser extent, every Member of Parliament is influenced in their attitude towards unusual events by their own personal experience. In early April my behaviour was dictated by a combination of personal experiences.

During my National Service, I had been tank crew with the Scots Greys in the British Army of the Rhine. Though never involved in actual fighting, 1950-52 was the time of the Korean War, and the possibility of combat was less than a far-fetched nightmare. Indeed, many of those with whom I did my basic training at Catterick and Aldershot, were sent to Korea. Some of them, among those who joined the Eighth King's Royal Irish Hussars, were badly shot up and never returned. Firing live ammunition and inhaling all the fumes in the turret of a Centurion tank was at least an experience which has made me feel that politicians should think twice before committing the members of their armed forces to military operations. It has seemed to me that, among leading politicians, those who were least enthusiastic in endorsing military action were precisely those who had 'a good war' in 1939-45 — for example, Carrington, Healey, Heath, Pym and Whitelaw. With some exceptions, such as John Silkin, who had been a naval officer in dangerous waters in World War II, those who most vehemently endorsed the task force were those who had never put on uniform, for whatever reason. I could barely control a smouldering anger at Mrs Thatcher's hawkish stance when I reflected that she had not only not been in the services but that Grantham, where she was brought up, had never been bombed. In particular, it stuck in my gullet every time she caringly referred to 'our boys' in the South Atlantic.

Some understanding of what battle actually involved was reinforced by a very clear conception of what angry seas could be like. For two years, 1961-62, I had worked on the Ship-School *Dunera*, the predecessor for British India Steam Navigation Company of the *Uganda*, which was to serve as the hospital ship of the task force. Having experienced bad weather in the Bay of Biscay and other places, I could imagine what the Roaring Forties would be like in winter in sub-

Antarctic conditions. The very idea of trying to land and take off Harrier aircraft on carrier decks in that kind of swell seemed hazardous in the extreme. At best, only partial and intermittent air-cover could be provided. I felt ships ought only to be sent on such an errand if the air-cover was total and continuous.

Now it might be contended that in the event my fears proved groundless and that in this respect my judgement was wrong. But was it? The Harrier pilots performed miracles of skill and human endurance. Yet, a third of the original Harrier force was lost. Air-cover was not provided. The witnesses to that appalling fact are in the burns units of hospitals in Britain, men of the Welsh Guards, in too dreadful a condition to be photographed when the Duke of Edinburgh visited them. Lt. David Tinker, RN, who died when a land-based Exocet missile hit HMS *Glamorgan*, wrote to his father on 22 May 1982: 'The Navy . . . overlooked the fact that we were fighting without all the necessary air cover which is provided by the USA in the Atlantic and by the RAF in the North Sea and Icelandic Sea. Although the Harrier is a marvellous little aircraft it is not a proper strike aircraft, and the best the Navy could get, when carriers were "abolished". Consequently, we have no proper carriers which can launch early-warning aircraft fitted with radar as strike aircraft. From the Fifties onwards these two were absolute essentials' (*A Message from the Falklands*, Junction Books, 1982).

One of my earliest childhood memories was the acute distress of my parents, when HMS *Prince of Wales* and HMS *Repulse* were sunk in 1941. This was the classic lesson that surface ships should not be hazarded against land-based air-power. Throughout April I was repeatedly to harp on about the problems of facing land-based air-power in the House of Commons. As we shall see later, the Prime Minister herself was mindful of the fate of the *Repulse* and the *Prince of Wales* and the lesson to be learnt from it.

However, on the logistical aspect, my central concern related to what advice had been given to Government ministers by their senior professional advisers, the Chiefs of Staff. Again, a personal experience prompted my almost obsessive concern about the nature of the advice which ministers had received.

When I was a new MP in the early 1960s, I used to visit an elderly relative of my father's. He was not very happy that I had become a politician and used to impress on me in clear, clipped terms that no politician had the moral right to over-rule the professional advice of Chiefs of Staff on matters that were clearly their domain. This elderly man in Banstead had been a Marshal of the Royal Air Force and, as General Eisenhower's Deputy, had been in close contact with many politicians of several countries. I took to heart the cogent lesson that Arthur Tedder, drawing on his own experiences, had taught me.

As soon as the assembly of·the task force was announced, I began to make discreet enquiries — the Government machine has become more leaky than it used to be — as to what on earth the Chiefs of Staff had said. The word I got back was that the Army was relatively content with its role, once a reasonably successful landing had been completed. The Navy wanted to go to the South Atlantic, not least to justify its belief that there was a future for capital ships of the kind the Government either wished to sell, like the aircraft carrier *Invincible*, or to scrap altogether. However, on the actual feasibility of conducting a successful operation at the end of an 8,000-mile supply line, the Navy were said to be less sanguine. (I had no notion then that possible losses were reckoned to include five major ships with many more badly damaged, let alone the losses, including possibly a carrier or major troopship, envisaged by Admiral of the Fleet Sir Terence Lewin in his speech to the Royal United Services Institution in June 1982.) It was what I heard of the attitude of the Air Staff which prompted my intervention in the House of Commons on 7 April: 'What advice was given to the Government by the Chiefs of Staff?' Then, eyeing Francis Pym, the new Foreign Secretary, and John Nott, the Defence Secretary, sitting a couple of yards away on the Government Front Bench, I added, 'I take it on my responsibility — every Hon. Member is responsible for his statements — to say that some Chiefs of Staff advised that the task force was not a feasible operation.' At that point, I offered to give way to either minister. When Mr Pym sank deeper into his seat and Mr Nott indicated that he had no wish to intervene, I added, 'The House is entitled to know what the Chiefs of Staff said to

Government on this issue. Some of us believe that the Fleet should turn round and come back to Portsmouth and Rosyth as soon as possible.'

It is inconceivable that, had they indeed had the backing of all the Chiefs of Staff, either Francis Pym or John Nott would have failed to jump down my throat. Francis Pym takes me seriously from the interminable hours during which he had, as Conservative Opposition Spokesman, to listen to me demolishing the Scotland and Wales Bills in the previous Parliament and John Nott does not hide the fact that he finds me a pain.

In actual fact, a few days later it was deliberately leaked to me that the Air Staff, alarmed about their reputation in the event of a military fiasco, wanted me to know, and say, that the task force had sailed against the advice of some, at least, of their most senior officers.

That the military situation did not go catastrophically awry was due to the skill and courage of our servicemen, together with a quite remarkable share of good fortune. On the other hand, if anyone had spelled out in early April that the British losses would be of the order that eventually occurred, many of those who gave their blessing to the despatch of the task force might have had second and third thoughts and preferred to turn the other cheek. In fact polls taken by ITV's 'Weekend World' on 8 April show that, whereas 61% of those polled strongly supported the use of 'diplomatic means backed by force', 57% were opposed to the loss of one British life in the exercise.

PART TWO: THE DEVELOPMENT

4. Parliament: the First Skirmishes

On Tuesday, 23rd March I gave lunch in the House of
Commons members' cafetaria to a talented young Leningrader,
Mikhail Bogdanov, the London correspondent of *Soviet
Industry*, to explain some of the Labour Party's attitude to
international scientific co-operation and other matters which
come within the orbit of Opposition Science Spokesman.
Suddently, there appeared on the closed-circuit TV that
informs us of House business, the notice of a statement—
'South Georgia incident'. My guest and I wondered what on
earth could have happened in South Georgia to warrant a
Commons statement and went on to discuss the Antarctic
Treaty. I mention this triviality to convey the fact that nine
days before the Prime Minister was to decide on despatching
an armada, few MPs, if any, had the least suspicion that there
was trouble brewing in the South Atlantic.

This contrasted markedly with the atmosphere on
2 December 1980. On a drab winter's afternoon the Honourable
Nicholas Ridley MP, then Minister of State at the Foreign
Office, subsequently translated to the Treasury, came to the
House of Commons to make a statement on his recent visit
to the Falkland Islands and consequential Government
proposals. I listened carefully to the statement, but remained
as mute as a Trappist.

At this point, I owe readers who are not familiar with
parliamentary procedure, an explanation. It is an understandable rule of government that no minister interferes in public
in the affairs of another ministerial colleague or his department.
Were this not so, it would be impossible to run any kind of
coherent government. The position of shadow ministers, who
are the opposite numbers of actual ministers, marking their
activities on behalf of the opposition, is a somewhat grey
area. Junior shadow spokesmen are allowed to intrude, within
reason, in the work of departments other than those for which
they have responsibility. My own position was complicated by
the fact that although I was a Senior Spokesman, I was also a
Shadow without a substance, in that there is no minister in
the present Government who is Minister of Science. The

Minister responsible for Science, the Prime Minister told me
in an official House of Commons answer, is herself; but I was
not Shadow Prime Minister! I dwell on this because at a later
stage Michael Foot felt obliged to sack me from being
Opposition Spokesman, on account of my public interventions
on the Falklands issue. Suffice it to say that in December
1980, a fortnight after being appointed to the Front Bench
after 19 years as an MP, I was certainly not disposed to
jeopardise my position, infuriate my colleagues and give
credence to those who had said that I was a 'loner' and not a
team player, by giving voice to my views on the Falklands.
Besides, in politics, there are often very personal and particular
reasons for doing or not doing things. As it happened, had I
spoken out then, there would have been jeering from some of
my parliamentary friends and ribaldry is lethal in politics.
The bizarre truth was that Jim Callaghan, exasperated by
my part in 47 days of opposition to the Labour Government's
Scotland and Wales Bill in 1977/78, had snapped, in the style
of Henry II asking his entourage 'Who will free me of this
turbulent priest' — that he wished he could send Tam Dalyell
far, far away — to be Governor of the Falklands!

'With permission, Mr Speaker,' began Nicholas Ridley, 'I
wish to make a statement on the Falkland Islands. We have
no doubt about our sovereignty over the Islands.' I was
immediately intrigued. This opening sentence was a 'termino-
logical inexactitude', a lie, as I was able to confirm later.
Ridley continued, 'The Argentines continue to press their
claim. The dispute is causing continuing uncertainty,
emigration and economic stagnation in the islands.' This I
knew was true. 'Following my exploratory talks with the
Argentines in April, the Government have been considering
possible ways of achieving a solution which would be acceptable to all parties. In this the essential is that we should be
guided by the wishes of the islanders themselves. Various
possible bases for seeking a negotiated settlement were discussed
These included both a way of freezing the dispute for a period
or exchanging the title of sovereignty against a long lease of
the islands back to Her Majesty's Government.'

I recollected that the Foreign Secretary, Lord Carrington,
had been quoted some days earlier, in November 1980, as
saying, 'The Argentines have got a claim on the sovereignty

of the Falkland Islands, which we dispute, and that claim is not going to go away.' The basic question at issue, as we have seen, concerned the legal status of the Falklands in 1833. Were they a no-man's-land, as claimed by Britain, or were they already under the control of Argentine as a result of rights inherited from Spain? Had Spain indeed controlled the Islands for a brief period during the 18th century?

But such doubts had no place in the minds of most MPs, particularly Mr Ridley's Conservative colleagues. My parliament-ary antennae are sensitive to tensions and they were registering gross indignation. To a background of muttering, Ridley affirmed, 'It is for the islanders to advise on which, if any, option should be explored in negotiations with the Argentines. I have asked them to let me have their views in due course. Any eventual settlement would have to be endorsed by the islanders and by the House.' I foresaw that the Minister was about to be savaged and that, to my distaste, the leader of the pack would be the Shadow Foreign Secretary, Peter Shore.

It is worth pausing to consider the political personality of Peter Shore, not least because in 1982 he was to play a pivotal role, albeit from another perch, as Shadow Chancellor of the Exchequer, in the formation of the Opposition's policy. This in turn was crucial in the unfolding of events, for without the support of the official Opposition in the House of Commons, I do not believe that even a Prime Minister of Mrs Margaret Thatcher's mulish obstinacy would have felt able to despatch the task force and still less inclined persistently to sabotage the various peace initiatives. Peter Shore is a man of consider-able intellect and thoughtfulness. Two decades ago, when we were both, together with Jack Jones, members of the Labour Party's Mikardo Committee on the Docks, I learned that Peter Shore was about the most skilful drafter of a document that I had ever seen in action. He was also one of the most effect-ive senior ministers in the last Labour Government, particularly as Secretary of State for the Environment. But on any given controversial issue in the field of Foreign Policy, I can be sure that Peter Shore and I will take diametrically opposing views. When I was chairman of the PLP Foreign Affairs Group and he was Shadow Foreign Secretary, twenty years of personal friendship was maintained but we held different viewpoints on sanctions against Iran, participation in the Moscow Olympics and the Soviet invasion of Afghanistan.

Though my heart sank, it came as no surprise in December 1980, when Peter Shore began: 'This is a very worrying statement.' Pointedly, Shore demanded to be told that the Minister would affirm that there was no question of proceeding with any proposal contrary to the wishes of the Falkland islanders. 'Their wishes are surely not just for "guidance"', I remember the mocking tone of that word which no repetition in print can convey, 'to the British Government. Surely they must be of paramount importance. Will Mr Ridley therefore make it clear that we shall uphold the rights of the islanders to continue to make a genuinely free choice about their future, that we shall not abandon them, and that in spite of all the logistical difficulties, we shall continue to support and sustain them?' The pattern of events leading to the abortion of the Ridley initiative was well and truly set. Indeed, with the benefit of hindsight, that was the moment when military conflict in the Falklands became inevitable.

Yes, said the minister, to all three of Shore's questions. With a deliberate ambiguity, which MPs can interpret as slyness—one of the most heinous crimes in the House of Commons—Ridley said, 'I confirm that our long standing commitment to their security and economic well-being remains, and I said that in the islands.'

The parliamentary fat was in the fire; the situation was irredemable. Shore had chosen the word 'paramount' to characterise the wishes of the islanders. It was starkly obvious that Ridley had deliberately sidestepped the notion of paramountcy. Later, in the Spring of 1982, after the Argentine military occupation, Mrs Thatcher was to exhume Shore's word 'paramount' and to repeat it again and again. It was a clever and legitimate tactic and one that firmly impaled the Opposition on her rapier. Paramountcy became part of the vocabulary of the whole Falklands crisis and it was Peter Shore, on that fateful December afternoon, who coined it.

What followed in the shape of parliamentary savaging cannot be fully understood without reference to aspects of the political character of Nicholas Ridley. The House of Commons is like a village, and villagers tend to react in certain ways to those with whom they have been brought up. It so happened

that Nick Ridley was head boy of Mr Tom Brocklebank's
House at Eton, and I have known him since he was 17 and I
was 12 years old. He is a man of outstanding intelligence and
considerable artistic ability, doubtless inherited from his
maternal grandfather, Sir Edward Lutyens the celebrated
architect. His father's family were Northumberland grandees.
As one of Edward Heath's Industry Ministers, responsible for
disagreeable decisions on shipyard closures, he was unloved
by many Labour MPs; as one who did not suffer fools gladly,
he was I suspect unloved by many of his own parliamentary
colleagues. To accuse Ridley of arrogance would be wide of
the mark. Rather, like other able men of his background, he
tends to become exceedingly perverse when attacked and
finds it hard to hide his impatience, if not scorn.

Things got off on the wrong foot that afternoon and went
from bad to worse. Sir Bernard Braine, stalwart of the Commonwealth Parliamentary Association, asked Ridley to agree that
the option of yielding on sovereignty and leasing back the
islands undermined a perfectly valid title in international law.
Even if he had tried, which his manner indicated was plainly
not his intention, Ridley could not have pacified Braine.
Russell Johnston, chairman of the Scottish Liberals, with all
the authority of the MP for Skye and sundry other islands,
asserted that Ridley's reception in the Falkland Islands left
the islanders in considerable doubt about his good intentions.
Was Ridley aware, asked the virtuous Johnston, that there
was 'no support at all in the Falkland Islands or in the House
for the shameful schemes of getting rid of these islands'
which had been, so he claimed, 'festering in the Foreign
Office for years?' Later in the exchange, I heard the
parliamentary Leader of my arch-opponents, the Scottish
National Party, tell the hapless Ridley that he should inform
the Argentine Government that the matter was closed, 'in
order to preserve the honour of the Government in the affair'.
Shortly afterwards, Mr Speaker Thomas, who himself for more
than a year as Minister of State in the Commonwealth Office,
had been responsible for policy on the Falkland Islands, called
James Johnson, the veteran Labour member for Kingston on
Hull, who, like Braine, Johnston, Stewart and others called,
were members of the Falkland Islands Committee. I clearly
recollect whispering out of the side of my mouth to a friend

and neighbour on the Front Bench, that this 'is all bloody well, but these folk ought to be telling us that they are members of the Falklands lobby'.

Not enough has yet been revealed about the activities of the Falklands Committee; for under one guise or another, it is they who have been instrumental in torpedoing Conservative and Labour attempts, in particular by Fred Mulley MP, to come to a rational solution on what is, after all, a fag-end of Empire. The Falkland Islands Committee started life as the Emergency Committee set up, in 1968, when it was thought that there might be a compromise reached with Argentina by the Labour Foreign Secretary Michael Stewart and other ministers such as George Thomas. Nine years later, in 1977, the Falkland Islands Office was set up, based in a somewhat pokey room adjoining the Willow Sandwich and Snack Bar, in Victoria. It is financed by sheep-farming companies, the Falkland Islands Company (latterly owned by Coalite) and sundry well-to-do islanders. Its lobbying position has been greatly helped by recruiting MPs who have been to the Falklands under the auspices of the Commonwealth Parliamentary Association. The Falkland Islands Committee give the impression of wanting to maintain the Falklands' 19th century position and way of life. Recent decades have witnessed the attainment of independence by most of Britain's former colonial territories, but this process of decolonisation – Harold Macmillan's 'wind of change policy' – has yet to reach the windswept Falkland Islands. Ironically, it was Macmillan's son-in-law Julian Amery, who formulated the most damaging question to Ridley. Saying that the statement was 'profoundly disturbing', Amery asked Ridley if he was aware that his department, the Foreign Office, had wanted to get rid of this commitment for years. Ridley was hurt. He replied that he thought Amery knew him well enough to realise that he did not embrace schemes thrust on him by his department. 'The Government as a whole has taken this initiative. It is of a political nature and it is not the job of the Foreign Office to devise such an initiative.'

Had the Government *as a whole* really taken this initiative? I mused. A very important component of the Government as a whole was the Lady in Downing Street. Had she really agreed? Perhaps she had. But it was mighty strange that one

of the 18 MPs who attacked the friendless Ridley had been
Mr William Shelton, Conservative MP for Streatham and Mrs
Thatcher's campaign manager in the leadership elections, in
which she and her friends hi-jacked the Conservative party
and ousted Mr Heath. Doubtless Mr Ridley and the other
Foreign Office ministers — Sir Ian Gilmour, Mr Douglas Hurd
and Lord Carrington, Old Etonians all — genuinely agreed with
the South American and NATO departments of the Foreign
Office — but did she? As we shall see, and as Julian Haviland,
Political Editor of *The Times* was perceptively to point out in
June 1982, so far as any lasting long-term solution for the
Falklands was concerned, there were chasm-like differences
between the Foreign Office and Downing Street.

It is impossible to prove conclusively, but my belief is that
had Peter Carrington been a member of the House of Commons
and not a peer in 'another place', the crucial outcome of
parliamentary events would have been different in December
1980, as surely as they would have been in the early days of
April 1982. Whereas a Minister of State at the Foreign Office
was fair game and an acceptable quarry for backbench hounds
to maul, given Tory party codes of conduct, it would have
been more difficult to maul a minister with a Foreign
Secretary sitting physically beside him, whom everyone knew
was committed to the policy. It would have been impossible
to maul one's own Foreign Secretary had he made the statement, as he would surely have done himself. Even Labour
MPs restrained themselves somewhat over Vietnam in dealing
with Michael Stewart. It is a psychological point, not
stemming from servility, but rather the knowledge that
injuring a senior minister in the Commons can put whole
governments at risk. Moreover, had Carrington been in day-to-
day contact with backbenchers that voting in the House of
Commons lobbies requires, he would have 'fixed' some of his
critics, made others see reason and certainly made sure that,
when a controversial statement was made, he had parliamentary friends jumping up and down to catch the Speaker's eye.
A Minister of State, however gifted, does not have the
authority or potential patronage to deal with these important
domestic chores. A Foreign Secretary has; he is considered
by many ambitious MPs to be important to them and they
will be happy to oblige him. Not for the first time, the

Foreign Office was to pay dearly for the honour of having a
peer as boss. No government is wise to have a very senior
minister in a sensitive job in the House of Lords. Besides, if a
Foreign Secretary is in the Commons answering MPs, it is
much more delicate and difficult, if not impossible, for a
Prime Minister to distance himself or herself from the
foreign policy of that minister. In December 1980, Mrs
Thatcher could view Ridley's parliamentary discomforture
with equanimity. Currently Financial Secretary to the
Treasury, Mr Ridley could be forgiven if he were to ponder
the thought that those MPs who with conspicuous relish
demolished his well-meaning proposals, got the war they
asked for and may indeed have wanted.

But the link between the collapse of the Ridley initiative
and the announcement by his successor Richard Luce on
23 March 1982 concerning the South Georgia incident was
by no means obvious, to begin with. My first impression was
that the incident was an escapade by assorted unauthorised
individuals which hardly warranted a statement in the House
of Commons and had been thereby blown up out of all
proportion. To this day, I suspect that this initial impression
was not wide of the mark. Luce began: 'I will with permission
make a brief statement on developments in South Georgia, a
Falkland Islands dependency.

'We were informed on 20 March by the commander of the
British Antarctic survey base at Grytviken on South Georgia
that a party of Argentines had landed at Leith harbour nearby.
The base commander informed the Argentine party that its
presence was illegal as it had not obtained his prior authority
for the landing. We immediately took the matter up with the
Argentine authorities in Buenos Aires and the Argentine
embassy in London and, following our approach, the ship and
most of the personnel left on 21 March. However, the base
commander has reported that a small number of men and some
equipment remain. We are therefore making arrangements to
ensure their early departure.'

Denis Healey, Shadow Foreign Secretary, then asked: 'Is it
not the case that the Argentine party planted an Argentine flag
on the island? Is it not odd that the right hon. gentleman did
not refer to that element? The Minister will recall that after
his talks with the Argentine representatives in New York

recently the Argentine Government said that unless they
obtained a satisfactory agreement they would take unilateral
action. Has the right hon. gentleman any evidence that the
recent actions of these Argentine citizens was in fulfilment
of that threat?'

To which Mr Luce replied: 'Yes, for a short period the
Argentine flag was planted. It has now been removed. We are
making arrangements to ensure that those who remain at
Leith harbour will not do so for very much longer.'

I confess to imagining that the Argentine flag had been
hoisted as if by football supporters; and, during the weekend,
I heard that a senior executive of Salveson's of Edinburgh,
the original owners of the wreck which had brought the
Argentine scrapmerchants to South Georgia in the first place
had jokingly said they were sorry for having caused trouble.
Little did we suspect that an opportunity would be afforded
by this incident and the way in which it was handled, to
create conditions for altogether less jocular matters.

5. South Georgia

By the following Tuesday, 30 March, a week after Luce's original statement, the sense of levity in the House of Commons had evaporated. A somewhat chastened Luce told us that 'the situation which has thus arisen, while not of our seeking, is potentially dangerous'. The Government had no wish to stand in the way of a normal commercial salvage contract, but the position of those carrying it out had to be properly authorised. It was clearly right to pursue a diplomatic solution to the problem, though the House would understand that he would rather say nothing about the precautionary measures. Denis Healey, while generally critical of the Government's unpreparedness and their policy of crippling the Royal Navy for the sake of the Trident Programme, contented himself with pointing out that a 'clapped out ice-breaker' like HMS *Endurance*, 'was no match for the five or six warships, armed with Exocet missiles, which the Argentine Government are reported to be sending towards the area'. Though Healey talked of a 'damaging humiliation in a situation that the Government should never have allowed to arise', he gave no hint at the end of March of wanting to go as far as military retaliation. Two back-bench interventions, in particular, should be noted, on account of the interveners' relationship to the Prime Minister. The first, succinct as ever, was by Enoch Powell: 'Is it the Government's view that public opinion in this country would support, if necessary, the use of force to maintain British sovereignty over the Falkland Islands and the dependencies?' The luckless Luce's response, earnestly hoping for a peaceful solution, was hardly of consequence. What was of enormous consequence was that Mrs Thatcher, who personally may have come late to the whole Falklands crisis (she was absent in Brussels on the day of Powell's question), must have realised with a thud that she might indeed be shamed into using or threatening to use military force.

At various times Tories have told me of the strange hold that Enoch Powell has over Margaret Thatcher, though probably they do not exchange a word in private. Some people scoff and ask how it can be. Personally, I understand very well how it can be. During some 47 days of parliamentary debate on Devolution, one and a half times the length of the India Bill in the 1930s, I sat in the chamber on the same side of the argument and hardly exchanged a word in the corridor with Enoch. Yet I confess that in all my endless speeches and interventions, I did rather crave for this intellectual approval and notice. I sense Mrs Thatcher suffers in the same mild way from being influenced, if not mesmerised, by Enoch's piercing, if often tragically wrong, intelligence. Considering the Powell/Thatcher relationship, I can comprehend how the Tsarina must have felt when confronted with Rasputin. Were the truth ever to be known, would it reveal that it was Enoch Powell's question that fertilised the seed of the task force?

The second major intervention, which would have been reported to the Prime Minister at least as soon as she returned from Brussels, was that by her predecessor, James Callaghan: 'I support the Government's attempts to solve the problem by diplomatic means, which is clearly the best and most sensible way of approaching the problem, but is the Minister aware that there have been other recent occasions when the Argentinians, when beset by internal troubles, have tried the same type of tactical diversion? Is the Minister aware that on a very recent occasion, of which I have full knowledge, Britain assembled ships which had been stationed in the Caribbean, Gibralter and in the Mediterranean, and stood them about 400 miles off the Falklands in support of HMS *Endurance*, and that when this fact became known, without fuss and publicity, a diplomatic solution followed? While I do not press the Minister on what is happening today, I trust that it is the same sort of action.'

Richard Luce replied: 'I am certain that the House and the Government listened to what the right hon. gentleman said with great respect. The Government note what he has said.'

Whether Margaret Thatcher respects James Callaghan I do not know. I suspect she does. What is an absolute certainty, however, is that she is not going to be seen as one whit less ready to use the Navy than 'Sailor Jim'. Mr Callaghan has always cared deeply about the Navy, in which he served in World War II and in which his father, a Chief Petty Officer, lost his life in World War I. Brought up in Portsmouth, James

Callaghan can at such times speak for millions of British people and those, like me, who do not share his opinions on the Falklands crisis, are forced to recognise that his gut reactions were those of many Labour voters and others in the country.

Impatient to move on to the next Commons statement of the day – ironically on the Death Grant levels – and subsequent business on the Gas Levy and Dental and Optical Charges – Mr Speaker Thomas called on Denis Healey for the last word. 'Is it not clear from the exchanges to which we have listened,' asked Healey, 'that the Government accept that the landing of the men in South Georgia was a deliberate provocation by the the Argentinian Government – for what purpose I do not know – and that it took place because the Government have not taken the sensible precaution of assembling adequate naval forces in the area as the Labour Government did in a similar situation? Will the Government learn from this experience that they must exercise more influence on the shape and deployment of our Armed Forces than they are doing at present? This is the first price that we are paying for a dreadful error in priorities in the Government's defence policy.'

The interesting point about Denis Healey's final word is that he avoided any hint that the Shadow Cabinet was thinking of endorsing the use of military force. Not long after he sat down, Denis Healey was aboard an aircraft on his way to the United States on a long prearranged visit, which had nothing to do with the crisis. He was therefore out of the country when news broke on Friday morning of Argentine troop landings in the Falklands. As so often happens in the course of moment-ous events, chance was to play a huge part. Unless Healey publishes particularly candid memoirs covering the point in detail, the world will probably never know for certain how Denis Healey would have reacted had he been in Britain on Friday, 2 April and Saturday, 3 April 1982. As one who had many differences of opinion with him in the 1960s, when he was Defence Secretary, over issues such as Anglo-French Variable Geometry Aircraft, the Borneo War, the use of Aldabra Atoll as an RAF staging post and chemical and biological weapons; and who did not vote for him as Deputy Leader of the Labour Party in 1981, my guess is that Denis Healey would have counselled his colleagues to display

reticence and caution, before committing themselves to
endorsing the use of military force. Denis Healey has travelled
widely, both as Defence Secretary and during a long stint as
Chancellor of the Exchequer. He has many, many foreign
friends. He knew Robert Alemann, the Argentine Finance
Minister. In younger days he had been a conspicuously brave
and much admired beach-master during the Allied Italian
landings in World War II.

If Denis Healey had been in London . . . is one of the *ifs*
of contemporary political history. He wasn't. But on the
morning of 2 April, when the Deputy Foreign Secretary,
the Lord Privy Seal, made an emergency statement in
the Commons about the Argentinian landing, John Silkin
was available, being MP for Deptford and a Londoner.
Whereas a Foreign Office statement ought to have been
answered by a Foreign Office Shadow Minister, it was in
fact answered by a Defence Shadow Minister—and, quite as
important, it was that Defence Shadow Minister who was
invited on to the BBC's 'World at One' programme.

It ought at this point to be said that the history of the
Falklands will be difficult for historians to piece together,
because so much that happened during the early stage was on
the telephone or on television, or often on radio. An historian
of the Crimean War, Ypres, El Alamein, Monte Cassino or
Korea even, could write a fairly complete narrative relying
on documentary evidence. In 1982, however, this is no longer
true. Any future history where the author has failed to
consult the numerous texts carried by Independent Radio
News, LBC, local radio stations like Radio Forth and Radio
Clyde, let alone the BBC, will present a woefully incomplete
picture of events as they occurred in Britain. Some
programmes were especially significant, such as 'The World
To-Night' and 'The World at One'.

Nothing said by any politician between April and June
1982 was more significant than the initial broadcast by the
representative of the Opposition immediately after the
Commons statement. Essentially what Silkin said, as
Opposition Spokesman, was that we should be prepared to
defend the Falklands 'even though it may mean fighting'
(see Appendix C, pp. 138-39, for full text of the interview).
The Government had got the green light: the official

Opposition would agree to the use of force.

It will be up to John Silkin one day to reveal in his memoirs whom he consulted before making what I believe to be a mis-judgement of historic proportions. (His will be among the more interesting political memoirs of the period from 1964 onwards, since he has been at the centre of events since the Wilson government of that year.) I know for a fact that he did not consult, for example, his Shadow Cabinet colleague and fellow left-winger Albert Booth, who has a long personal history of interest in Defence. Michael Foot subsequently defended John Silkin vehemently to me when I made the implicitly offensive suggestion that Foot had been cornered into the position of supporting military action against his will, by the public utterances of Silkin. Indeed, whether consulted or not, I can only now suppose that Michael Foot concurred with Silkin's judgement out of conviction and not simply out of chivalrous loyalty to a friend and senior colleague. Yet I do think this episode on 'The World at One' on 2 April is a prime example of how policy can be instantly made in a broadcasting studio. Indeed, I have some sympathy with John Silkin and others, once they have allowed themselves to be lured into a studio. The temptation to be not indecisive is very powerful. When Brian Widlake launched his final question, 'And we must defend them in your view even though it may mean fighting?', John Silkin had decided to be decisive. 'Certainly,' said he. From that moment, the parliamentary Labour Party leadership was on a motorway which perhaps it never really intended to travel, but from which there was no obvious exit. All-party support for military action was in the bag.

Like most other MPs, unaware of the speed at which events were moving, I had gone home to my West Lothian constituency and was having lunch in the kitchen with my wife when we heard Silkin's ominous words. So alarmed was I that I hastened to my phone, tried to get through to John Silkin and eventually tracked down Anne Carleton, his personal assistant, who phoned back to say that my worries 'had been overtaken by events'. I wasn't so sure. John Silkin had been my friend for 20 years and I knew that like many Jewish Socialists he was passionately opposed to anything labelled 'fascism', passionately in favour of protecting British people against the excesses of

Europeans (or, I imagined, people in South America of Latin stock) and passionately against anything smelling of aggression. My difference with him was simply that I did not think that he understood much about South America or knew much about the background to this particular dispute. I therefore cancelled all constituency engagements, in readiness for a return journey to London, and determined to try to get a word in Michael Foot's ear the next day, Saturday, 3rd April.

6. Emergency Debate, 3rd April

On countless occasions during the next ten weeks the Prime
Minister, Mr John Nott and Mr Cecil Parkinson, Conservative
Party Chairman and member of the War Cabinet, lost no
opportunity of reminding the British people and the world
of one central fact. It was the House of Commons as a whole
that had willed the task force. Had it not been so, the fleet
would not have sailed. Let us therefore dwell at length on
just what happened to provide substance for the assertion
that the task force was the creation of the House of Commons,
not just of Her Britannic Majesty's Government.

Timing in life is often decisive. Argentinian occupation
was learned about on a Friday. Thus the House had to
assemble on a Saturday—the first Saturday session since
Suez, a quarter of a century earlier. Certain considerations
were no less important for being mundane. A significant
number of leading MPs had speaking engagements on the
Saturday night. They would have to get home or to the parts
of the country where they were speaking. It would be
difficult for many members from the North of England to
catch trains to get them to Westminster by 11 a.m. The last
shuttle flight to Scotland left at 5.40 p.m. from Heathrow on
Saturday, not 7.40 p.m. as on weekdays. Thus it was decided
by the 'usual channels', that is, the Leader of the House and
Shadow Leader of the House and a bevy of whips—that the
debate should last from 11 a.m. to 2 p.m., to create a minimum
of personal inconvenience. There was a valiant effort, led by
David Stoddart (Lab., Swindon), to get the debate extended
by a couple of hours (which, as a colleague put it, was 'all
damn well for a man whose home was in Reading'). However,
after a vote on this, which took up more time out of the
allocation, the three-hour span was agreed.

The debate was opened by a tense Prime Minister. Mrs
Thatcher told a packed House that by late afternoon the
previous day, it had become clear that an Argentine invasion
had taken place and that the lawful British government of the
islands had been usurped. She said that she was sure the whole
House would join her in unreservedly condemning 'this

unprovoked aggression by the Government of Argentine
against British territory. It has not a shred of justification
and not a scrap of legality'. The Government had decided
that a large task force should now sail as soon as all prepar-
ations were complete. 'I stress that I cannot foretell what
orders the task force will receive as it proceeds. That will
depend on the situation at the time. Meanwhile, we hope
that our continuing diplomatic efforts, helped by our many
friends will meet with success.' At this point I interrupted her
speech with the question already referred to, 'Have we any
friends in South America on this issue?' Mrs Thatcher
responded that doubtless our friends in South America
would make their views known during any proceedings at the
Security Council. She added, 'I believe that many countries
in South America will be prepared to condemn the invasion
of the Falkland Islands by force'.

As Leader of the Opposition, Michael Foot followed the
Prime Minister. He asserted that the rights and the circumstances of the people in the Falklands must be uppermost in
the minds of MPs, though there was no question of any
colonial dependence 'or anything of the sort'. It was a
question of people who wished to be associated with this
country, who had indeed built their whole lives on the basis
of association with this country. 'We have a moral duty, a
political duty and every other kind of duty to ensure that
this is sustained.' Any guarantee from this invading force was
utterly worthless—'as worthless as any of the guarantees that
are given by this same Argentine junta to its own people'.

According to the hallowed traditions of the House, Mr
Speaker Thomas had little option other than to call a proces-
sion of senior Privy Councillors. Edward du Cann, chairman
of the Conservative Back-Bench 1922 Committee, was
astounded that for all our defence expenditure, 'which in
absolute and proportional terms is huge, and for all our
capacity for diplomatic activity and intelligence, we appear
to have been so woefully ill-prepared'. He asked the House to
resolve that our duty was now to repossess our possessions,
and to rescue our own people. For Enoch Powell, there was
only one reaction which was appropriate to meet unprovoked
aggression upon one's sovereign territory: that was 'direct
and unqualified and immediate willingness—not merely

willingness expressed by action—to use force'. Nothing should cast doubt upon their will and intention to do it. Looking Mrs Thatcher full in the eye, Mr Powell concluded: 'The Prime Minister, shortly after she came into office, received a soubriquet as the "Iron Lady". It arose in the context of remarks she made about defence against the Soviet Union and its allies: but there is no reason to suppose that the Right Honourable Lady did not welcome, and, indeed, take pride in that description. In the next week or two this House, the nation, and the Right Honourable Lady herself will learn of what metal she is made'. In view of the store which Mrs Thatcher sets by having Mr Powell's good opinion, this was an important moment.

Sir Nigel Fisher, the veteran MP for Surbiton, biographer of Ian MacLeod and Harold Macmillan, believed that the very least we should do was to ensure the exclusion of Argentina from the World Cup. In the cacophony of demands for drastic action, no one excelled the former Foreign Secretary and then Social Democratic Party parliamentary leader, Dr David Owen. When I asked him to give way, Dr Owen replied: 'No. There is no question of anyone in the House weakening the stance of the Government'. His response revealed the extent to which many MPs had shut their minds to argument. Julian Amery, erstwhile minister and Suez rebel, scorned compromise. Ted Rowlands, former Labour Foreign Office minister responsible for the Falkland Islands, said that he had a god-daughter in Port Stanley and charged the Defence Secretary and the Foreign Secretary to restore to the islanders their rights, safety and security as urgently as possible. Patrick Cormack, Conservative MP for South West Staffordshire, said the Government had blundered. Former Labour Commonwealth Secretary at the time of Ian Smith's declaration of UDI in Rhodesia, Arthur Bottomley, asked that as long as the inhabitants wanted to remain in the Commonwealth, Britain should see that they should do so.

The first jarring note was introduced by Ray Whitney, chairman of the Conservative Party Foreign Affairs Group who, in an earlier career had been a diplomat in Buenos Aires. Whitney was concerned about the effect of the use of military force on very substantial Anglo-Argentinian community and with the practicality of either a sea and air blockade or a military landing.

Never in over twenty years as a member of the House of Commons, have I witnessed Tory members of Parliament round on a colleague, suggesting that he was simply a Foreign Office 'apologist' – the politest of a motley collection of intemperate words used in my hearing. The venom directed towards the Foreign Office was epitomised by a former President of the Board of Trade in the Wilson Government, Douglas Jay, who thought that they were 'too much saturated with the spirit of appeasement' and by Sir John Eden, former Conservative Industry Minister, who claimed that he had long suspected elements in the Foreign Office of trying to get rid of what they regarded as a tiresome problem. Sir Bernard Braine, Conservative, Russell Johnston, Liberal, and Donald Stewart, Scottish Nationalist, all members of the Falkland Islands Committee, made unusually bellicose speeches. Bravely, George Foulkes, South Ayrshire, called at the fag-end of the debate, came out firmly against military action. Though a number of us were clamouring to catch the Speaker's eye to put a dissentient point of view, Foulkes alone got the chance to make a speech. The gist of what he said was that his 'gut reaction was to use force', but that 'we must also be sure that we shall not kill thousands of people in the use of that force'.

Winding up for the Opposition, the Shadow Defence Secretary, John Silkin, referred to the Argentinian President as 'this present bargain-basement Mussolini, Galtieri'. This phrase was hardly calculated to make subsequent negotiations easier. Name-calling never does. I learned later that the impression given to Argentinians was that many members of the House of Commons thought of them as inferior 'dagos'. This, according to an Argentinian friend of mine in Britain, infuriated many people in Argentina who did not love Galtieri, but did not like to hear foreigners calling him names.

As I have already suggested, the House is very much like a village; we all know each other and have a long history of relationships with each other. When some prominent villagers slip up they tend to get more sympathy than others. Those who get least sympathy are those senior ministers who are thought to have behaved|wilfully or arrogantly in the past. In this category came the Defence Secretary, John Nott. He

it was thought had been off-hand and aloof towards his
critics, particularly when they had protested about his plans
to proceed with Trident at the expense of conventional
forces. Indeed he had been brutal towards certain MPs
having Navy interests, or dockyards in their constituencies,
and the peremptory dismissal of Keith Speed, MP for Ashford
and a junior Navy minister who had publicly protested against
proposed cuts in the RN were very fresh in the villagers'
memories. There was no way that Saturday morning in which
Mr Nott could have satisfied Parliament. Mr Nott got into
deep trouble when he was interrupted by a former Tory
minister, Eldon Griffiths, who firmly plunged the knife in
by saying that he spoke as one of the Defence Secretary's
'supporters'. 'Understanding full well, as I do, the psychological difficulties of a large surface fleet, why did he not put
the hunter-killer submarines on station two weeks ago?' John
Nott did not attempt to answer immediately, and never
recovered. He slumped deeper into the mire of parliamentary
failure. The need to redeem his reputation became itself a
significant factor in the equation of compromise or
determination to win during the weeks that followed. The
only way of exorcising the memory of that parliamentary
débâcle was to come back to the House with tidings of
military victory. In the War Cabinet, Nott's was to be a voice
against compromise. As Mr Nott sat down, battered and
sheepish, *Hansard* records, 'It being two o'clock, Mr Speaker
adjourned the House without Question being put, pursuant
to the Order this day'. The 'usual channels' had agreed that
since Parliament had been recalled on Saturday, no vote should
be taken. Had a vote been allowed under the rules, my
impression is that quite a number of MPs who were reluctant
to criticise once the fleet had actually sailed, would have
been prepared to cast their vote against the sending of a
task force which had not then left harbour.

   Another important factor to be considered is that, had the
debate lasted six hours, the normal time allotted on a routine
parliamentary day, it would have been neither so tightly
packed with MPs, nor so highly-charged. The hysteria,
acknowledged by seasoned parliamentary observers in the
Press Gallery as unique in their experience, would not have
become so combustible. As usual, MPs would have walked out

after the opening speeches. Without doubt more junior MPs would have been called and questions about logistics would have been raised. (I tried to interrupt David Owen, as I have shown, to ask how long we could sustain a war in the sub-Antarctic. Normally he would have felt bound to give way, but in view of the time allowed each speaker he was unwilling to do so.) In other words, doubts would have surfaced.

Now it may legitimately be asked: If there were so few overt doubters about the task force during the following week, how can it be suggested that there were many sceptics on that Saturday, April 3rd? There is a simple answer. Once the task force was seen assembled on television by the electors, few MPs wished to be seen in the position of 'not backing our boys'. There is another partial explanation for the apparent unanimity of the House of Commons. Many MPs did not attend the emergency debate since they did not wish to cancel their usual Saturday morning 'surgeries'. Nor is this a matter to sneer at. If an MP has advertised that he will be at a certain place at a certain time to meet any of his constituents who wish to see him, he is expected to be there, come what may. (Had my own 'surgery' that Saturday been at a location other than Whitburn, where Councillors Alec Bell, Danny Flannigan and Bert Gamble were more than happy to help me out by seeing constituents, I should have thought twice before going to London.) There were some Left-wing MPs, like Bob Cryer and Denis Skinner, who might have objected to the sending of the task force and voiced their disapproval, if only by shouting and heckling. However these MPs were just those most likely to be committed to political engagements on a Saturday afternoon, at demonstrations or marches. It would never have occurred to them to be absent during an official parliamentary weekday.

Once the approval of the House of Commons had been given to the task force, it was difficult for those who either had not been present or who had not voiced their objection, to criticise the decision to send it. On Saturday, 3 April the Government used the House and made its members prisoners in pursuit of what by then some of their leading members wanted to do—to fight a war. If it is true that sending a military expedition to the Falklands suited President Galtieri, it is equally true that some Government ministers saw a war in the Falklands as a welcome distraction from British domestic problems. However, many more, like the Leader of the Opposition, men of peace, fervently hoped that the task force they had sent would never be used in anger.

Since he made a speech of profound consequence and since his attitude was to be a matter of utmost importance in the coming weeks, it is to Michael Foot that we must now turn. For I am convinced that it was a central part of Mrs Thatcher's strategy from an early stage to trap the Labour Party in general and its leader in particular in her net, so that there could be no escape if things went wrong. She was going to make sure that those who lent themselves to the despatch of the task force should also lend themselves to its use. The first steps in any war are easy. On Saturday morning, before he made his speech, I was able to waylay Michael Foot briefly to express my anxiety about the reaction in Latin America and to warn him of the formidable nature of Argentinian arms, many of which, like Exocet, had been bought in Europe. (Like Denis Healey I thought that Buenos Aires had surface-to-surface ship-launched Exocet: I had no notion that they had managed to fuse Exocet to the wing of an aircraft.) Charming as ever in listening to his colleagues, Michael Foot had clearly made up his mind about his speech. It was to be a great oration by a great Commons' orator, equalled possibly only by Iain MacLeod in the last 20 years. Many of my colleagues were ecstatic. And, as a political speech, I suppose it was an impressive performance. Younger MPs, who had never been near a battlefield, roared approval. 'Michael has shown us that he can be Prime Minister, which I did not believe until this morning,' said one. But it seemed based firmly on the widely-held assumption that the task force would never be used in earnest—and about that I held a different opinion and was therefore as stunned as many of my colleagues were ecstatic.

When Foot declaimed: 'There is no question in the Falkland Islands of any colonial dependence or anything of the sort', I remembered how sensitive 230 million South Americans were to the colonial issue. Moreover, according to the *Oxford English Dictionary*, a settlement in which the settlers retain a political connection with their home country is a colony. Thus it seems the Falklands *are* a colony and are so perceived throughout Latin America. As Roberto Campos, the Brazilian Ambassador, was to put it to me, 'Do you British really care about the sensitivities of 1,800 Falkland islanders more than the sensitivities of 230 million others?' Furthermore, it occurred to me that my Leader, a not inconsiderable historian, ought to have understood the effect of their history on South Americans. Emancipation from European Princes was the very stuff of their history and here we British were agreeing with the Prime Minister that HMS *Invincible* 'will be in the lead and will leave port on Monday'. I suppose Prince Andrew had to go with his ship, but the idea of a European Prince sailing into the Western hemisphere in the 1980s was anathema. Michael Foot went on: 'It is a question of people who wish to be associated with this country and who have built their whole lives on the basis of association with this country. We have a moral duty, a political duty and every other kind of duty to ensure that this is sustained'. Maybe in theory, but in practice I knew that we had not even coughed up the £12 million which the Shackleton Committee said was needed and, furthermore, the lives of the younger Falklanders were becoming, for education and other reasons, more and more dependent on Argentina. 'The people of the Falkland Islands have an absolute right to look to us at this moment of their desperate plight, just as they have looked to us over the past 150 years.' Were this the whole story, what on earth had we, as Labour and Conservative governments, been doing to reach an accommodation with Argentina over the past 17 years? 'Any guarantee from this invading force is utterly worthless — as worthless as any of the guarantees that are given by the same Argentine junta to its own people.' If this were true, why was a Labour Government selling them Type 42 destroyers? Though at least a Labour Government had cut back on arms that were most suitable for repression. 'We can hardly forget that thousands of innocent people fighting for their political rights in Argentina are in prison and have been tortured and debased.' True, but I suspected that on the issue of the Malvinas, even they would follow the light blue and white flag. Officially the Montanneros did support the junta. 'We cannot forget that fact when our friends and fellow citizens in the Falkland Islands are suffering as they are at the moment.' Suffering or not, the House of Commons and

all speakers ought also to have been thinking about 17,000
British passport holders in Argentina itself, to say nothing of
100,000 'Anglo-Argentines'. Perhaps the obligations of the
British Government towards the Falklanders are qualitatively
different from and greater than their obligations to the
British subjects and persons of British descent living in
Argentina. Yet numbers do matter. Does anyone imagine that
the world would have thought the same of Hitler if he had
put six Jews, and not six million Jews, to death?

Michael Foot was rightly concerned to emphasise the
United Nations' role. Certainly, in the early stages, partly due
to the skilful work of Sir Anthony Parsons and his colleagues,
with whom I had spent a week the previous year as an official
Labour delegate, we had UN sympathy on the original
aggression and a favourable vote in the Security Council.
More note should have been taken of the fact that the one
country to vote against us in the Security Council was
Panama—the only Hispanic American state involved and the
one who was most interested in the issue. But the key to
Michael Foot's speech was in the peroration: 'I return to
what I said at the start of my remarks. We are paramountly
concerned, like, I am sure, the bulk of the House—I am sure
that the country is also concerned—about what we can do to
protect those who rightly and naturally look to us for
protection. So far, they have been betrayed. The responsibility
for the betrayal rests with the Government. The Government
must now prove by deeds—they will never be able to do it by
words—that they are not responsible for the betrayal and
that they cannot be faced with that charge. That is the charge,
I believe, that lies against them. Even though the position and
the circumstances of the people who live in the Falkland
Islands are uppermost in our minds—it would be outrageous
if that were not the case—there is the longer term interest
to ensure that foul and brutal aggression does not succeed
in our world. If it does, there will be a danger not merely to
the Falkland Islands, but to people all over this dangerous
planet.'

Herein lies the key to Foot's attitude. It is simply not fair
to sneer as some have done at the hollowness of his peace-
mongering. I believe there is an explanation. In his early man-
hood—and those of pensionable age often tend to return to

the concerns of their youth—Michael Foot wrote a deservedly famous polemic, *Guilty Men*. This contained a withering attack on Chamberlain and his circle for not standing up to fascist dictators, particularly Hitler. Foot obviously felt that the Argentine invasion of the Falklands had a parallel with the 1930s. Yet Leopoldo Galtieri was not Benito Mussolini, let alone Adolf Hitler. Argentina presented no kind of threat to us, as Nazi Germany had. Indeed, until the Falklands battle, Argentina had never been involved in a war in its history, other than a comic skirmish with some Paraguayans. Yet here were we British bringing war to the South Atlantic which, apart from the naval battle of the Falkland Islands in 1914, had not known war. However, Michael Foot's speech had been so successful on the Government side that Mr Patrick Cormack moved to say 'that he truly spoke for Britain'. My worst forebodings were confirmed. Michael Foot, for whom I had voted in every ballot as Leader of the Party and whom I wanted very much to succeed, would not be allowed to wriggle out of the clutches of the bellicose MPs all around.

There is, however, a question for the Labour Party that has ramifications far beyond the actions or personality of Michael Foot. How, after the endless party agonising on the general principles of accountability, did it happen that the most crucial decision by a British government in a quarter of a century came to be endorsed by the parliamentary leadership of the Opposition, with a minimum of consultation? It is not an adequate answer for the Opposition leadership to plead that they were forced to make up their minds on 2nd April and 3rd April. It would have been perfectly honourable to have postponed endorsement of the task force until at least a meeting of the parliamentary labour party and the National Executive Committee of the Labour Party had taken place.

Now it may be said that both these bodies, and other senior ruling councils in the Trade Union movement were to support their initial gut reaction. What, however, is by no means obvious is that the initial reaction would have been the same if there had been adequate opportunity for reflection and if there had been no question of disowning the Party Leader and the Defence Spokesman: in other words, if the argument had been about the merits of the case. It is my firm belief that had the Opposition declined to endorse the sending of the task force, even Mrs Thatcher would not have embarked on so unlikely an adventure, given that the country was visibly divided on the issue.

I shall be surprised if the various constituent bodies of the Labour Party allow the matter to pass. Many members will see the Party's actions in the Falklands' hour of decision as yet another reason why accountability of the leadership is vitally necessary. For the inescapable fact is that, whatever public opinion polls may have said and whatever Labour voters may have thought (and that is doubtful), the majority of active members of the Party, who do the day-to-day work of the Party, were out of tune with the Shadow Cabinet.

7. Another Point of View

Given the highly-charged emotions of the electorate, it is understandable that MPs should have been coy about making public statements as to whether or not they supported the idea of sending a task force before they had consulted their constituency parties. Time was not on their side in this unique set of circumstances. In most controversial matters there is ample time for consultation, if there is a will to consult. Not so in this case. Out of the blue the task force would be sailing on Monday, 5 April, a mere 48 hours after the decision was announced in the House of Commons. Most politicians were just not able to meet their constituency associations at such short notice. Therefore they said nothing. Silence was taken for acquiescence, if not consent. Having acquiesced, men of integrity felt that, whatever their misgivings, they were obliged to go along with supporting the task force. As I have suggested, the issue immediately became blurred, since from Monday, 5 April the main concern of the British public ceased to be the merits or demerits of despatching a task force and became one of support for our fighting men.

The television pictures of young troops with their kit filing on to troopships to the accompaniment of bands and cheering or sobbing women, transformed the debate from one of 'what should we do' to 'how will the task force do it'. Argument about the rationale for going at all was swept into the background. The fact that George Foulkes, Judith Hart and I felt free to speak out daily during the following weeks urging the recall of the task force was due, in large measure, to the fact that we had publicly objected to the sending of the force at the first possible opportunity on 2nd and 3rd April.

I was lucky too in that the monthly meeting of West Lothian Constituency Labour Party fell on Sunday, 4 April. At these meeting I give a parliamentary report and make it a practice to raise those issues on which there might be potential disagreement between the constituency party and myself. Mutual candour leads to a trusting relationship. For the first time in 20 years I phoned the Secretary of the CLP, asking

that precedence be given to my parliamentary report, as I
wished to raise in detail the whole issue of the Falkland
Islands and what had occurred during the previous day's
Commons debate. Bill Gilby readily agreed. I should explain
that West Lothian CLP is large and well-organised. It has on
its General Committee a substantial number of politically
serious men and women with responsible positions in public
life, whose opinions I genuinely value. After I had outlined the
events of the previous 48 hours, Councillor Donald Stavert,
the chairman of the CLP, put the legitimate and proper
question, 'All right, Tam, what would you have done if you
had been Foreign Secretary?' I repeat from my diary notes
what I said:

I would myself, as Foreign Secretary, have gone to Buenos
Aires, accompanied not only by senior diplomats but by the
Director of the British Antarctic Survey, Dr Lawers, together
with a number of eminent geophysicists and marine biologists
and would have said this to General Galtieri:

'You would not expect us to say that we approve of the
military landing in the Falklands/Malvinas. But, you know
and we know that military action would be out of all proportion to any argument between us. Further, we know and
you know, that talk of economic sanctions is preposterous in
a situation where your neighbours, like Brazil, for the past
149 years have officially recognised the Malvinas as part of
Argentina and would be happy to help you evade sanctions.
Other than a skirmish with Paraguay, you have never fought
a war and there has been a history of friendship between our
two countries ever since we helped you become independent
of Spain.

'Frankly, we are not at all clear what the position of the
Malvinas is, in international law. We concede that in the 1830s
Britain did take the Malvinas from the Spanish Empire and
there were the dubious activities of Samuel Lafone and others.
Our Foreign Office knows of some embarrassing documents,
which purport to uphold the claim of Argentina, and we concede that the authoritative work on the subject *The Struggle
for the Falklands* by the American academic Jules Goebel
(1927) comes down on the Argentinian side of the argument,
on the basis of the doctrine of *uti possidetis*, recognised throughout Latin America.

'So, President Galtieri, in the knowledge that you have many pressures on your home front, which prompted you to jump the gun in the takeover of the Malvinas—it was going to happen anyway—and in the knowledge that your Junta shows signs of trying to do something for the "disappeared ones", the victims of preceding governments, we should like to put three questions to you.

'First, will you allow those English-speaking people, some of whom we admit are second-class citizens of the UK under our Nationality Acts, to have the same rights, in relation to language and culture, as the Scottish and rugger-playing Welsh communities of rural Argentina?'

The answer would have been, 'Of course, Foreign Secretary, they shall have the same rights. Since there are no roads outside Port Stanley and you have been unable to find the £12 million for infrastructure suggested by your 1976 Shackleton Committee, we think driving on the left or right-hand-side of dirt tracks is not a momentous issue. Nor do we think it a great hardship to instruct the young in the Spanish language since many of them come to school in Buenos Aires, or come here for hospital treatment.'

'Secondly, President, there are some—possibly a few—who will wish to leave the islands. Can we agree on some fair compensation terms?'

'Yes, we can agree that anyone who wants to leave is free to do so. But we must point out that your Shackleton Committee found that one-quarter of the farms and 46% of the land is externally owned, much of it by people in the pressure group called the Falkland Islands Company. This is owned by Coalite, who have won over a number of your MPs. People who are more English than the English ought to have their home in the Thames Valley, where they spend most of the year in any case. We can work something out on compensation. However, we will distribute land to those who remain who, until now, have been little more than company serfs, dependent on the Company for their livelihood.'

'Thirdly, President, are you willing to guarantee the work of the British Antarctic Survey and the well-being of the scientists? Further, could we not extend scientific co-operation between Argentina and Britain in the sub-Antarctic? We would point out to you that many Argentinians have distinguished themselves at British universities and, indeed, your César Milstein at the MRC Laboratories in Cambridge led the team that developed the enormously important monoclonal antibodies. Now I have Dr Lawers and his colleagues here. Perhaps they could discuss an agreement? We know that the Malvinas are an extension of the South American continental shelf, but you know that South Georgia and the South Sandwich Islands are geologically different. None the less we ought both to put our minds to the winning of resources by the signatories of the Antarctic Treaty.'

The answer in Buenos Aires, would have been 'Delighted. We look forward to doing battle with you in the World Football Cup in Spain'.

The next speaker after myself was John Barclay of the Fauldhouse Labour Party, an ex-serviceman, who expressed doubts about my position on the grounds that we should perhaps 'back our boys' and that we must stand up to Fascism. (A fortnight later John dropped me a generous note: 'You were right and I was wrong!') Then, as often happens at CLPs, there was a powerful and clinching intervention. Jack Cunningham, ex-Secretary of the Fire Brigades' Union in Scotland, is a trade union heavyweight. He has impeccable anti-Fascist credentials, but he argued that for Britain to go to war in the 20th century over islands that we had never cared about was another matter. Last week, he asked, how many people in this county of West Lothian were absolutely sure where the Falkland Islands were? The Party leadership should never have backed Mrs Thatcher on this and what were the TUC General Council doing? The trouble was, Cunningham observed, that too many working-class people, particularly in the South, put jingoism before Socialism. It was the Labour Party's duty to take a stand against this. Councillor Allister Mackie, leader of the Labour group on West Lothian District Council, also talked about the duty to resist jingoism for, like many others, he had been appalled by hearing extracts from the Commons emergency debate live on radio. Councillor Alec Bell, vice convenor of Lothian Region Council, moved that their MP be given a free hand in opposing the sending of the task force. This motion was seconded by Councillor Mackie, who drew attention to what he foresaw as the colossal costs of the Falklands armada,

which he contrasted with the miserable cuts he was currently
obliged to make as chairman of the Manpower Services
Committee of Lothian Region. When we have the local
authority manual workers, the hospital workers and many
others being grossly underpaid, in a country that cannot
invest properly in its railways (West Lothian CLP benefits
from the fact that I am a National Union of Railwaymen-
sponsored MP), how can we afford to make war in the South
Atlantic?

I do not pretend that I would have changed my mind on
the task force if West Lothian CLP had reacted differently.
Their backing, however, was of enormous psychological
importance. It gave me, as it would any MP, confidence to
campaign within the Party in the knowledge that I was
voicing the views of those without whose work I would not
be a Member of Parliament at all.

8. Cocks and Carrington

On Monday, 5 April I arrived post haste from Scotland and
my first port of call was the office of the Opposition Chief
Whip, Michael Cocks. Whereas in the Tory Party there is
something of the hierarchy that one might expect in industry
or the forces, relationships in the Labour Party with the
whips are informal and friendly. Besides, Michael Cocks is my
old office room-mate and we have been friends for many
years. So the picture of me storming into his office in high
dudgeon to suggest that he go to Michael Foot, to tell him
that he had better accept the resignation of his Science
Spokesman, is quite unreal. My attitude was simply, 'Look,
Michael, I'm aghast at what the Leadership are doing in
relation to the task force. All that is in me reacts violently
against this course of action, which I conceive to be disastrous
for the country and, incidentally, a heads-you-win-tails-I-lose
situation for the Labour Party.' I then gave him a detailed
explanation, to which he listened patiently. However, I could
sense that he thought his old friend was 'over the top', if not
out of his mind, in his upset over sending the task force. To
show that I was serious, I said to him, 'Don't you think you
ought to go to Michael Foot and tell him that if he wants my
resignation as Science Spokesman, he has only to give the
word. I've worked hard at this job and would hate to give it
up, but . . .' What was interesting was Michael Cocks's reaction,
not my offer of resignation. 'Don't be daft! This thing won't
last! It would be stupid to give up your job on the Opposition
Front Bench for something that will leave the centre of the
political stage as rapidly as it came.' This was meant in the
nicest possible way. What it revealed was that the Labour
leadership, like most other people in Britain, believed that it
would never come to any kind of battle and that the dispute
with Argentina would be solved peacefully through diplomatic
negotiation. Therefore there was no point in any Opposition
politician going to the stake for a cause which he could do
nothing about and which was going to resolve itself anyway. I
thought differently. To be fair to Michael Cocks, it is true that
the speed of the action on 5 April was for effect. The build-up

for real operations was less theatrical and less publicised.

Once on a moving staircase how do you get off it? Specifically, at what point could the Opposition, having agreed to the sending of the task force, turn round and say, 'Thus far and no further!' That was the question that neither Michael Cocks on that early Monday morning, nor anyone else at Westminster was ever able to answer. The basic reason why they never really applied their minds to it was partly to be found in what I call the 'disbelief factor'. Most MPs thought that fighting simply could not take place. In the second half of the 20th century it was inconceivable that nations which had been friends over the years could come to blows. Mr MacCawber was present and an eager participant whenever Labour MPs discussed the question of the Falklands throughout April and a good deal of May. Something would surely turn up. The Americans would not allow it. Did we not believe in the miraculous healing powers of Al Haig, the then American Secretary of State? Could we imagine Casper Weinberger, the US Defence Secretary, allowing two of his major military allies to risk lives and equipment needed by the West and to go for each other's throats in earnest? Would Helmut Schmidt not do something, with all those German-Argentinian contacts? Or would there not be a remarkable personal initiative by that well-placed gentleman from Peru with the unpronouncable name (Senor Peres de Quella), the UN Secretary General, who was so widely trusted in Latin America? And if the UN Secretary General and the US Secretary of State did not have miraculous powers, there was always Pope John Paul II, he of immense personal authority?

The hard reality was, of course, that with every nautical mile the armada covered, the harder it was to get people to say that it should return. I vividly recollect going onto Independent Radio News on Monday, 5 April to be questioned on why I was reported in the morning newspapers as having said the task force was 'the most ill-conceived expedition to have left these shores, since the Duke of Buckingham set sail for La Rochelle in 1627'. Towards the end of my interrogation I was asked, 'So, Mr Dalyell, what would you actually have the Government do now?' — a very reasonable question from Mr Peter Murphy of ITN. 'Turn round in the Solent and go back to Portsmouth and Rosyth,' said I. One of my not unsympathetic friends in the PLP heard this on his car radio as he was travelling to the House of Commons: 'But you can't do that!' he said, 'It's too late.' Thought, such as there was among 600 or more MPs, was of the haziest. The fleet would not get beyond the Western Approaches; the Argentinians would give way when they saw we were serious. Well, at least, the fleet would stop at the Azores and the lads would have a good training exercise. Ascension Island then became a favourite stopping place. Even uncompromising opponents of the sending of the task force were to agree that it was reasonable that the fleet should remain at Ascension Island. Then there was a school of thought, articulated and repeated by Merlyn Rees, former Home Secretary and close friend of James Callaghan, that the fleet should go for South Georgia. I was one of the very few who tried to persuade our colleagues that we were inexorably to be drawn into costly island-storming warfare such as that undertaken by the Americans at Guadalcanal, Iwagima and the Solomon Islands in World War II. Thankfully I exaggerated, in that the losses did not turn out in the event to be of Pacific proportions.

But on Monday, 5 April, Westminster was very much in the world of hope and miracles, until people's interest was distracted by the news that Lord Carrington had resigned and that Mr John Nott had not resigned. During the afternoon, at Question Time, it became clear that something was brewing. It so happened that I asked the Lord President, Francis Pym, the following question: 'Did the Lord President advise the Foreign Secretary and the Defence Secretary that, as soon as the first shot was fired, they would be taking on right, left and centre the entire Spanish-speaking world, including many of those who have suffered at the hands of Right-wing Governments and who still believe that the Malvinas, or Falkland Islands, belong to a South American State 400 miles away, not a European State 8,000 miles away?'

Pym sat transfixed and though normally the most courteous of parliamentary performers, declined to answer. I wondered if his refusal to respond was that he could not easily go along and advise himself in his new capacity as Foreign Secretary!

To return to Lord Carrington's resignation, however, the circumstances are of more than usual interest and the whole

truth may not be known, even to an Enquiry or to those who
will come to write the authoritative work on the Falklands'
affair. One thing is certain and the rest is informed conjecture.
The certainty is that, just as in December 1980, at the time of
the Ridley initiative, the outcome would have been different
if the Foreign Secretary had been a member of the House of
Commons, so, 17 months later, the Tory back-benchers would
not have been allowed to run riot against the Foreign Office
if an authoritative and prestigious Foreign Secretary such as
Carrington had been present. I am told by Conservative MPs
that they doubted whether, as a busy, globe-trotting Cabinet
Minister, he had ever spoken personally to half his colleagues
in the Commons. He was therefore in no position to defend
himself, his junior ministers, Humphrey Atkins and Richard
Luce, who resigned with him, or his Department. One effect
of the Falklands affair is that no Prime Minister in the foreseeable future is likely to appoint a minister in a sensitive
office of state from the House of Lords.

It will not do to simplify matters, as some have done, by
saying that Carrington resigned because he felt that the
Foreign Office had blundered and the Government had to
find a scapegoat. An ex-Guards officer of Carrington's
experience does not leave his post at the beginning of a crisis.
As Dick Crossman's Parliamentary Private Secretary I had
been involved on the fringes of the negotiations about Lords
Reform in the 1960s, when Crossman was Leader of the
House and Carrington was the leading Tory peer. All I knew
of him, then and since, suggested that he would certainly not
quit because the going got rough. It was just not in character.

Entering the world of conjecture, there were two reasons
why Carrington might resign, or a combination of both. Either
he did not believe in the policy of sending the task force,
holding it to be an over-reaction to what Argentina had done,
or he had been double-crossed by his colleagues. I find it inconceivable that neither the Foreign Office nor the Intelligence
Services knew some weeks before 2 April that there was a
strong possibility of an Argentinian military assault on the
Falklands some time before the 150th anniversary of the
British occupation of the islands in 1833. After all, they had
only to read *Clarin* and other newspapers close to the
Argentinian military to find this out. Perhaps they did not

predict that the assault would take place so soon, for the
simple reason that not until the unscheduled, unanticipated
farce on South Georgia with the Davidoff salvage episode did
the rulers in Buenos Aires decide to take advantage of the
situation. Even then there is some evidence that it was done
by Admiral Inaya and his satrapy without the prior knowledge
of President Galtieri. If the Argentine Government did not
know the timing, it is rather severe to blame the Foreign
Office for not getting the timing right! However, some military
attack, sometime, was expected. The Foreign Office must
have known this. I suggest that some people in the Foreign
Office—rightly, in my opinion—shrugged their shoulders and
agreed that being presented with a *fait accompli* was probably
the best thing that could happen, since there was no way
either of defending those intransigent Falkland islanders in
perpetuity, or of persuading them to reach an accommodation
on sovereignty with Argentina which, since November 1980,
Lord Carrington had recognised as a problem that would 'not
go away'. Nor do I suppose that officials kept this intelligent
view to themselves. Nor were they, or should they have been
ashamed of it. It is more than likely that Peter Carrington
shared this general view of the Falklands—when his mind was
not on the EEC, the Middle East, Southern Africa and a host
of other problems. After all, what were Britain's long-term
interests in the South Atlantic? Patriotic Foreign Office
officials could say that our real interests were threefold and
that they coincided with the real interests of the Falkland
islanders: first, peace in the South Atlantic, secondly
international control of Antarctica, in the interests of con-
servation, scientific investigation and the rational exploitation
of renewable and non-renewable resources; thirdly, good
relations with the Latin American comity of nations, based
on understanding and mutual benefit. However, from the
South American viewpoint all these interests were jeopardised
by what was perceived to be a British colonial presence on
South Atlantic islands and the British conflict with Argentina.
I must make it clear that I have no friends or friendly moles
in any area of the Foreign Office remotely dealing with Latin
America at the present time and have no axe to grind on their
behalf.

One vital question which arises is, did Carrington convey

his views on the Falklands to Mrs Thatcher, who is very much
concerned with national glory? It is possible that he did not.
I have the impression that the Prime Minister's attitude,
unlike Heath's and Wilson's, is 'Don't bother me until I have
to make a decision or things come to a head'. She does seem
to wait until problems have become acute and then charge at
them — a view of her ways widely shared in Brussels.

However, it is altogether more likely that Carrington did
keep Mrs Thatcher fully informed. I offer two separate pieces
of circumstantial evidence. First, not only has Richard Luce,
his Minister of State at the Foreign Office, repeatedly implied
that he has nothing to fear from an enquiry, but Foreign
Office officials pressed for an enquiry, in the expectation
that they would emerge from it unblemished. For me there is
another scrap of evidence of far deeper significance. For
twenty years I have known Robert Rhodes James, first as
one of the young Clerks of the House of Commons and,
since 1973, as Member of Parliament for the City of Cambridge.
He is the author of a famous Life of Lord Rosebery, which
reveals a great reverence for accuracy (since Dalmeny,
Rosebery's home containing the family papers is in my West
Lothian constituency, I feel reasonably well qualified to say
this). Rhodes James was Parliamentary Private Secretary to
Nicholas Ridley, when Ridley was Minister of State at the
Foreign Office and one of the few MPs close to Peter
Carrington. When, on 20 June, it was put to him by an interviewer on LBC that 'the public has been given to understand
that the Foreign Office was to blame', Rhodes James replied,
'I know differently'. It is unlikely that this was an unconsidered
remark from a man who was in a position to know and assess
the truth. If, therefore, the Foreign Office was not to blame,
the finger of suspicion must point towards Downing Street.

Here lies the second scrap of circumstantial evidence. As
James Callaghan said on 7 April in the House: 'Of course the
Foreign Office and the Ministry of Defence receive the
telegrams and the intelligence assessments, but so does the
Prime Minister. Every week, she has all the major telegrams,
all the intelligence assessments and, if she wishes, the raw
material on which those assessments are made. If I may say
so to the right hon. Lady, they are for her guidance. It is for
her to use her judgement on the information that is put before

her, and on this occasion she made a gross blunder. I know that Conservative Members always throw a protective cloak around the Prime Minister when she is attacked, but it is necessary to question her past in this matter if we are to consider what part she is to play in the future'. The fact is that the Prime Minister of the day receives a special box every Friday, which alerts him or her to worrying problems that could easily 'blow up'. I cannot believe that both the Foreign Office and the Intelligence Services would have been so sure of their own position, to refrain from informing Mrs Thatcher. My view is that she did indeed know and that one of two things was uppermost in her mind. She thought either that the take-over of the Falklands by Argentina would be a nine-day wonder, which the British Parliament and people would accept wearily as inevitable or there would be a fight. The former is more likely. When, however, the Argentinians did actually invade the islands, they produced a political whirlwind, in which the Conservative back benchers and many other MPs fed on the tabloid press and other more respectable papers, and in which the press in turn fed on the hysteria of MPs. Mrs Thatcher was then able uninhibitedly to declare war.

It is a grave charge to make against a Parliamentary colleague, let alone the Prime Minister of one's country, but she herself did let this particular cat out of the bag when she addressed the Annual Scottish Conservative Party Conference on 8 May: 'What really has thrilled me — having spent so much of my lifetime in Parliament talking about things like inflation, social security benefits, housing problems, environmental problems and so on — is that when it really comes to the test what thrilled people wasn't these things. What thrilled people was once again being able to serve a great cause, the cause of freedom. (Applause) They don't necessarily fight for a country because they want more wages, higher benefits and new international economic order — anything like that — but because it's a free country'.

The astonished Scottish Press Corps were taken aback that she could so clearly imply that she preferred dealing with great issues of principle like the Falklands, to questions of economics and social security. Moreover, though she was genuinely downcast and dejected, even crumpled, on the night she had to come to the House of Commons and sit

John Nott while he announced that HMS *Sheffield* had been sunk, for most of the time she gave the clear impression of being highly elated by her presence on the centre of the world stage, involved in a cause which she had almost instantly come to see in stark black and white terms. I am not necessarily suggesting she actually wanted a fight from the very beginning: I am saying that she was not averse to it, if it were to be the easiest option.

I submit that when Carrington realised that his Prime Minister—about whom he already had many reservations—declined to allow events to come to a head in the South Atlantic to the advantage of Argentina, he decided he would have no part in a military conflict and resigned. Such an explanation of events tallies with the Prime Minister's request that he should remain in Office and squares with his determination to leave and cultivate his garden. With Lord Carrington's departure went the last hope that the British Government would reach an accommodation. Henceforth it was more than coincidence that at every stage when a settlement looked possible, the Government appeared to throw a spanner in the works. For example, we retook South Georgia on the eve of a crucial meeting of the Organisation of American States, and we sank the *Belgrano*, as we shall see, just when it looked as if the UN Secretary General was about to reach a mutually honourable compromise. If our actions were not by design, then they were very clumsy.

9. An Interview with Mrs Thatcher

If an air of bewilderment at what was portrayed nightly on television pervaded Buenos Aires, it was also present in the House of Commons. There is a sensible rule that Party meetings are only reported to the press by the chairman of the Parliamentary Labour Party, so I cannot give details of the formulative PLP meeting on the morning of Wednesday, 7 April, other than to record what appeared in the newspapers. As the *Financial Times* reported, the meeting was on the whole prepared to support the Government. Michael Foot was warmly applauded for suggesting that in certain circumstances force was justified: 'I am not a pacifist and I have always supported the United Nations.' Indeed, support for the UN was the most frequent refrain among those MPs who contributed to the discussion. To dissent from the use of force was to play into the hands of Galtieri and other like-minded dictators. The Labour Party was urged to stand together: the disunity of the Opposition, alone, could save a discredited Prime Minister. Subsequently, Tony Benn predicted that any military exercise would end in tragedy, and Labour should not be seen to lend support to a doomed Prime Minister in a doomed enterprise. Giles Radice, MP for Bishop Auckland, spoke for many colleagues when he called for 'no blank cheques and no moral gestures'. As the chairman rightly said, my longish argument about lack of air cover and the Argentines seeing the Malvinas as part of their nation, whereas the British saw it as a property to which we had a right — was received with attention but widespread disagreement. Denis Skinner also remarked to me on leaving the meeting, 'You told them the truth, but don't kid yourself, most of the PLP simply did not agree with you!'

Basically, the difficulty was that only four days after the task force had been launched, the dispute had become one of a struggle of wills between Britain and Argentina and had ceased to be an argument on the merits of the case. Many weeks later, on 30 June, the reporters Robert Fox and Brian Hanrachan were to say of their experience with the task force, 'There was no point in discussing whether we should be there

at all' and went on to observe that the task force were not
upset by dissident voices on programmes such as 'Panorama',
but by the publication of details of troop movements. I must
repeat my contention that, once the task force had gone,
many people thought that there was no point in discussing
whether it should have gone. The adventure gathered
a momentum of its own.

Secondly, there were some highly respected MPs, like Stan
Newens, who had consistently campaigned for twenty years on
Latin American issues, but who supported the sending of the
task force. In early April, they said they were not in favour of
retaking the islands by force, did not take an uncompromising
stand on the issue of sovereignty and had not suddenly
become raving jingoists or supporters of gun-boat diplomacy.
For them the issue of self-determination was at stake and
they were concerned about the need to make a stand in
other parts of the Third World. Newens had defended the
right of the people of East Timor to resist the Indonesians
and had justified the presence of Cuban troops in Angola to
resist the South Africans. Newens felt that those who had
taken his position would be in serious danger of being justly
accused of adopting double standards, if they were now to
write off the Falkland islanders whose presence there was
'an historical accident'. Any community had a right to
determine their own future and he was seriously disturbed
by the fact that so many people who had upheld this principle
elsewhere did not seem to think that it applied equally in the
case of the Falklands. Newens's argument weighed heavily
with the leadership of the Labour Party. My response was
that those who accepted that the Falkland Islands were a
colonial relic could surely agree to seek a non-colonial future
for the islands. The brutal reality was that neither full
integration into the United Kingdom, which the Falkland
Islands Committee appeared to want, nor full nationhood of
the kind given to Guyana and Belize, were viable permanent
solutions. In any case, as it turned out, the Thatcher Government were not prepared to give all Falklanders full British
nationality. The real political cowardice of the last twenty
years had been not to spell this out, either to the Falkland
islanders or to the British electorate. We were now paying
for the consequences of this political failure and lack of

foresight. I refused to concede that territorial rights could ultimately be decided by 1,800 people, an implanted population, the majority of whose members were dependent on landowners resident in Britain, in particular the Coalite Company. In other words, numbers *do* make a difference. It is also important whether the population is indigenous or not. In my view, the democratic rights of the Falkland islanders could have been guaranteed and entrenched under an agreement with the Argentine, which would at any time in April have been underwritten by the Americans or the United Nations or both. *De facto*, there would have been local self-government, as in the remote areas of Patagonia. (This is precisely what a number of Labour Members of the Latin American Group of the National Executive Committee wanted in 1976/78.) What we had to face up to as Socialists, I argued, was that we would never get a credible Latin American policy so long as we retained colonies in the region. Those MPs who infuriated me at the beginning of April—and they were from all sides of the House, some even from the Labour leadership—were the advocates of sending ships and troops, but reserving their position over the use of the task force. It seemed to me highly insensitive to suggest that men in troopships should loiter round the South Atlantic in arctic weather conditions indefinitely. It was ridiculous to suggest that we could say to troops, 'We've sent you to the South Atlantic, but of course we forbid you to fire a shot in anger or to get yourselves fired upon.' The bluff would have been called and the nation would have looked ridiculous. (This attitude is not a matter of hindsight: it was spelled out clearly by me on 7 April.) It can never be proved one way or the other but I am inclined to think that the Parliamentary calendar, having played a significant part in despatching the task force on Saturday, 3 April, again brought negative influence to bear on events through the Easter recess. During the week, 12-17 April, all that Parliament did was to meet on Wednesday, 14th for a debate. As Judith Hart put it to me, 'if you want to start a war, choose a weekend, and if you want to make demonstrations against war impossible, choose Easter week!' As I have said before, timing can be everything.

I suggested to those Labour MPs opposed to the further progress of the task force that we should meet at 11 a.m. on

Wednesday, 14 April, in Committee Room 10. This was to prove a grave error on my part. I ought to have realised that with Commons Business starting at 2.30 p.m., few MPs would arrive from the North in a recess much before 1 o'clock. In addition, many who were sympathetic did not know of the meeting. The result was a turnout of only eleven MPs. However, this by no means reflected our strength at that time, which was at least fivefold. The meeting was brief and confined to our tactics in opposing the Government. The veteran left-wing MP, Frank Allaun, a member of the NEC and former chairman of the Party, insisted that we make our position crystal clear to Michael Foot. When Judith Hart and I went to see Michael Foot to do this, he naturally asked how many had attended the meeting. So did Denis Healey, when Judith and I met him in the passage leading from Foot's room. We could be discounted with impunity.

At the afternoon debate which followed our private meeting on 14 April, the running was made by Denis Healey, who argued that every possibility of a diplomatic settlement should be explored. The Security Council should be discussing the British Government's proposals, not those of the Russians or of someone else. If we were seen to be responsible for bloodshed and carnage, our international support, such as it was, would melt away – a prophecy which was to prove accurate in the event, when a 9 : 1 majority in the UN became a 1 : 9 minority. However, Healey also insisted that we must maintain our present position for the removal of Argentine troops. Many of us were unable to see how this objective could possibly be achieved without bloodshed. Douglas Hoyle, a member of the NEC of the Labour Party, and recent by-election winner at Warrington, called on us to face up to the prospect of military action and took the view that we could not support such a course. I thought that the most effective way of making Parliament concentrate its corporate mind on the reality of the situation was to raise the question of air superiority, given the obvious advantage that a land based air power traditionally has over naval forces. I therefore asked the Prime Minister: 'Am I right in thinking that if the task force arrives off the Falklands there will be sufficient air cover against a land-based air force from the Argentine?' To which Mrs Thatcher replied: 'I shall have something to say about air cover in a moment. I have every confidence in all aspects of this task force.' Then later in the debate I again asked the Prime Minister: 'Before the right hon. Lady comes to the end of her speech, I wish to repeat my question about air power. Does the right hon. Lady not remember what happened to *Prince of Wales* and *Repulse*? Does she not know that there are at least 68 Skyhawks as well as the Mirages and R5-30s in the Argentine Air Force? That is a formidable force, if the task force is to go near the Falkland Islands. Will the right hon. Lady answer my question?'

Mrs Thatcher replied: 'I have indicated to the hon. Member for West Lothian and to the House that we have taken steps to double the provision of the Harriers. We believe that that will provide the air cover that the hon. Gentleman and the House seek. I trust that he and the House will express confidence in our naval, marine and air forces. That is what they are at least entitled to have from the House.'

By the time Parliament returned on 19 April from the Easter recess, the cheerful confidence shown by many MPs before the recess had begun to fade. It had now become evident that the Argentines were not going to cut and run simply because the British fleet was on the distant horizon. Furthermore, they looked as if they might be able to invoke the Intra-American Treaty of Mutual Assistance, which was a chilling prospect both for Britain and the then American Secretary of State, Al Haig. On 21 April, I set out carefully prepared views to Labour colleagues, which are significant for the response they evoked.

'Politicians who press servicemen into courses of action, when the means of carrying out those courses of action to a successful conclusion are doubtful, have an awesome responsibility and must risk daunting criticism at the bar of history, when the bill has to be paid in other people's lives and in the world standing of one's country. In a campaign like the Falklands, you have to distinguish between what you want to do and your capacity to do it. Invading the Falklands: do we have the means? It is an MP's duty to warn of the loss of life and possibly a defeat of the first magnitude. The task force has been spatchcocked together at the shortest notice and details have been announced as titbits for the media, without regard to immediate need or to long-term relevance.

It was improvised for objectives which are ill-defined and may
be impossible to fulfil. Al Haig has said that a military
solution will not provide a lasting solution. Yet the Opposition
are being sucked into complicity in trying to obtain a military
solution. Now a lasting military solution might be possible.
But for how long would the British people be willing to be
stuck with a commitment of indefinite duration and increas-
ing expense? It could end like the Russo-Japanese War, with
Britain in the role of the Russians at the end of a long supply
line; or, like Dieppe, 1942, when fixed defences were attacked.
It is all very well for Michael Foot to say that he hopes for as
swift and successful an action as possible, but we have to
look, unlike leading Liberal Russell Johnston who thought it
could be done without loss—at the facts. The Argentinian
Marine Corps officers and men are highly thought of by their
professional colleagues in Britain and the United States and
could fight well. [This turned out to be true.] The conscripts
could fight as if they were in a holy war. [This turned out to
be false.] They have a hundred 105 mm self-propelled anti-
tank guns and Austrian Kurassian tanks, modified for dirt-
track conditions. They have 300 infantry carrying vehicles,
capable of bouncing round the terrain, and towed howitzers.
This is not a rag-bag force to be despised. The Navy have 3
submarines, 2 diesel-electric Kiel-built, lying somewhere dogo
in the Atlantic, with the awful prospect of attacking the thin-
skinned *Canberra*. The Navy has surface-to-surface missiles.
The Argentine Air Force has Skyhawks and Mirages with
R-530s, that deadly combination in the hands of the Israelis.
Their mines at sea could be devastating and we are sending
ex-fishing boats, with metallic not wooden or plastic hulls,
as minesweepers. It does nothing but honour to our forces to
say that they are up against troops who are highly professional,
in spite of their appearance on film like military peacocks.
Don't we now have to say that faced with the stark reality of
a war where we are friendless, that we advocate the withdrawal
of the task force to home ports, which might indeed enhance
rather than detract from the negotiations at the United
Nations?'

Denis Healey thought it was absurd to suggest that withdrawal of the task force would help UN negotiations, but I
remain unconvinced. At that stage it might have done, since

the Falklands were in the world spotlight and Argentina
would have saved face. It is perhaps worth reflecting that
'face' plays a large part in the Latin temperament and indeed
in Mrs Thatcher's makeup, too. The official Labour strategy
was to concentrate on helping the perceived 'doves' in the
War Cabinet, Pym and Whitelaw, against the majority hawks,
Thatcher, Nott and Parkinson. Since Pym and Whitelaw were
clearly not willing to offer a joint threat of resignation and
actually mean it, I saw no point in gearing our policy to trying
to help them. They were not going to win.

However, I was interested to guage Mrs Thatcher's mood on
this point. Indeed, it was one of the reasons why I took up her
public offer to Roy Jenkins of an interview with any MP who
wished to see her. (I understand that the number of MPs who
accepted her challenge could be counted on one hand.) To her
credit she saw me at 9.30 p.m., the same day my request
reached her. Most courteous she was too, receiving me with
the quip, 'I have always got time to see the awkward squad'.
I came away convinced that whatever Pym, Whitelaw and
others of Denis Healey's 'doves' may have desired, the lady
who mattered believed that the crux of the Government's
case was that the use of armed force must not seem to be
rewarded. Therefore, whatever others may have thought – or
Pym, Whitelaw, *et al.* may not have thought, because I'm not
as sure as Healey that they were pedigree doves at all! – she
would not compromise in giving Argentina even the most
minimal of concessions that it needed.

10. An Act of Naked Aggression

After the task force had set sail on 5 April it journeyed
steadily south until a segment reached South Georgia which it
retook from Argentinian marines on 25 April. On 1 May a
Vulcan bomber based on Ascension Island and refuelled in
flight struck at Stanley airstrip. In most British people's
minds, however, the Falklands conflict was still only shadow
boxing. The sinking of the Argentinian cruiser, *General
Belgrano*, on 2 May changed all that and the war slipped
from second into fifth gear. The conflict escalated out of all
proportion. There is little doubt that the Exocet attack on
HMS *Sheffield* on 4 May was retribution for the attack on
the *Belgrano*.

Meanwhile Mrs Thatcher was ostensibly carrying on peace
negotiations. After the breakdown of the US Secretary of
State, Al Haig's, peace 'shuttle', hopes of negotiations were
in the hands of the Peruvian Government and the UN
Secretary General, Perez de Quella.

To this day Britain is suspected by Peru and other Latin
American countries of not really wanting meaningful negotiations with Argentina until a military victory had been
secured. The Peruvian President, Fernando Belaunde Terry,
has accused Britain of direct responsibility for the collapse
of the Peruvian mediation effort by sinking the *Belgrano* – a
decision which we now know from Admiral of the Fleet Sir
Terence Lewin, and from the returning Captain of HMS
Conqueror, the submarine that launched the torpedoes, was
taken in London and not by the Commander on the spot,
under 'rules of engagement'.

The gist of the Peruvian plan transmitted by Foreign
Minister, Arias Stella, to US Ambassador Frank Ortiz in
Lima, was as follows: (1) a period of truce; (2) mutual withdrawal of military and naval forces; (3) an immediate opening
of negotiations between Britain and Argentina with reference
to past UN General Assembly Resolutions on the Falklands
(which urged progress towards 'decolonisation' of the islands,
while respecting the islanders' interests) and to the meeting
of the Organisation of American States (which recognised

Argentina's rights to sovereignty, though not its actual sovereignty); and (4) temporary administration of the islands by the United Nations, with the support of an international peace-keeping force. The

The Americans let Downing Street know of these proposals, which were eminently reasonable for a British Prime Minister who was anxious to avoid war. Downing Street demurred. The Prime Minister was not satisfied. So Haig and Belaunde set to work together and put together a modified seven-point plan: (1) an immediate cessation of hostilities; (2) mutual withdrawal of armed forces; (3) the installation of representatives from countries other than the parties involved, to govern the islands temporarily; (4) the British and Argentinian Governments would recognise the existence of differing and conflicting claims over the Falkland Islands; the two Governments would recognise that the viewpoint and interests of the islanders must be taken into account in seeking a peaceful solution to the problem; (6) the contact group which would immediately intervene in the negotiations to put this agreement into effect would consist of Brazil, Peru, West Germany and the United States; and (7) before 30 April 1983, a definitive agreement would have to be reached under the responsibility of the four countries.

Once again, timing played an important part. The Peruvians knew that Francis Pym was in Washington that weekend. They had reason to believe that these proposals constituted at least an acceptable basis of negotiation to the Foreign Secretary and his advisers. So, late on Saturday evening, 1 May, President Belaunde in Lima telephoned President Galtieri in Buenos Aires. The Argentine President consulted the Junta and called Lima back in the early hours of Sunday, 2 May, with a number of proposed modifications, particularly in relation to the interests of the islanders, which he accepted, and their 'viewpoint' which he did not. He also suggested that someone other than the United States, perhaps Italy or Mexico, should be the fourth member of the contact group.

I have been told on reliable authority that there were a large number of phone calls on that Sunday, 2 May, between Washington, Lima, Buenos Aires, and at least two from Washington to London, though I was not told who answered in London. Points 4, 5 and 6 were amended as follows: (4) the two Governments recognise the existence of differing and conflicting claims over the Falkland Islands, and will take account of the resolutions on the islands approved by various international bodies; (5) the two Governments recognise that the aspirations and interests of the local inhabitants must be taken into account in the definitive solution of the problem; and (6) the contact group which would intervene immediately in the negotiations to implement this agreement would be composed of various countries to be designated by common agreement.

The Peruvians and the Americans now thought that peace was assured. On Sunday afternoon, Lima time, President Belaunde actually went on television to claim that his mediation was going to be successful. In the early evening, Belaunde received a phone call from a furious Galtieri saying that, just as they were putting the finishing touches to a decision to approve the proposals, terrible news had been received. The cruiser *Belgrano* had been torpedoed with heavy loss of life.

When she gave the order to Admiral Sir Terence Lewin at the London Naval headquarters in Northwood to allow the Commander of *Conqueror* to launch his torpedoes, the Right Honourable Mrs Margaret Thatcher, PC, MP, must have known full well how close she was to being offered a basis for peace, which she could not reasonably refuse. Which, if any, of her colleagues knew, it is difficult to say. I guess that Francis Pym in New York did indeed know how close an acceptable settlement was, but was not consulted about the decision to fire the torpedoes at *Belgrano* just as he was sitting down to a working dinner with Perez de Quella. In fact I have been told, by sources close to the US Defence Secretary, Caspar Weinberger, whom Pym talked to at length in Washington on the Sunday morning, 2 May, that no indication whatever had been given of the intention to sink a major Argentinian ship.

There was no real justification offered for the sinking of the *Belgrano*, which shocked Latin America with the huge loss of life in the Antarctic waters. The most usual comment offered by ministers at this point was epitomised by John Nott, saying on television on 9 May, 'In twenty years time they will say, "The British stopped aggression"'. The most apt reply to this crass explanation of the escalation of the war

was that it did not prevent Mr Begin from going into the
Lebanon with a vengeance, less than twenty days afterwards.
Indeed, when the history books of the period come to be
written, I should not wonder if the worst aspect of the
Falklands crisis may not be that it distracted American
attention from the Middle East. This may well have allowed
the Israelis to assume that they could launch a massive
offensive against the PLO with impunity. After all, Mr Begin
did claim before the television cameras of the world, that he
was only doing in the Lebanon what Mrs Thatcher was doing
in the Falklands.

The day after Mr Nott referred to Britain 'stopping
aggression,' Sir Anthony Parsons, our Ambassador at the
UN, described his efforts as those of a 'man driving around in
the fog; it could be sunshine next, or it could be a brick wall.'
Having spent a week with Sir Anthony and his colleagues in
the British Mission to the United Nations in 1980, I know
how influential a figure he is at the UN, and was not
surprised when somehow or another he won a decisive vote for
Britain at the beginning of the conflict. However, like many
others on this side of the Atlantic, I believed that on several
occasions Sir Anthony came within a stone's-throw of an
honourable settlement, only to see it evade him as a result of
intransigence in London.

What we noticed was the number of occasions on which
Sir Anthony Parsons in New York and Sir Nicholas Henderson,
our Ambassador in Washington, went onto American television
to stress that the task force had the backing of almost the
whole House of Commons and the British people. This was
one of the reasons why some of us thought it essential to call
a vote against the adjournment to the debate on the night of
Thursday, 20 May. Another reason for our decision was that
Mrs Thatcher gave warning on 14 May, on television, that a
peaceful solution to the conflict might not be possible and
indeed on 19 May the UN peace initiative finally died. There
had been no meaningful attempt to come together with the
Argentinians. On the contrary, the fighting had continued to
escalate, with the bombardment of the Falklands on 9 May
from sea and air and the landing of Marines on Pebble Island
on 15 May. On the day of the debate, on 20 May, without
hearing what the House had to say, the Prime Minister

ordered the British task force into battle.

But there were other reasons why my colleagues and I decided to vote against the adjournment to the debate on 20 May. At the beginning of the Falklands crisis, we had been told that full international support was a *sine qua non* for Britain sending a military task force. Both front benches had agreed that the views of the international community were of the utmost importance – though as Michael Foot once put it, when he was on the back benches, 'When both front benches are agreed in British politics on a controversial issue, they are almost certainly likely to be wrong'. But by the middle of May, the situation was as Andrew Faulds described it: 'We started this unhappy operation with a large degree of world-wide support following Argentina's illegal occupation. We have already seen that support drain away as a result, in the first place, of our naval operations, and particularly the sinking of the *Belgrano*. The Hispanic world has declared its support for Argentina. That is not surprising – it shares the same sort of memories of Spain's colonial exercises in South America.

'The United States administration have shown obvious concern about our intention to settle the twentieth century problem of decolonisation by nineteenth century means. We have gravely jeopardised America's relations with the whole of South America. Whether we believe that those relations were pursuing sensible courses or not, we have gravely jeopardised the possibility of the leading power in the world influencing what happens in South America, whether for good or ill.

'Our European colleagues have expressed their reservations – to put it mildly – about the Government's military intentions.

'The EEC action, in disregarding the Luxembourg compromise, is both a signal of how fed up our European colleagues are with the fabricated toughness of the Prime Minister, and a mark of disapproval for, if I may term it such, the Thatcher tantrum exercise in the South Atlantic, which is apparently, inevitably and inexorably leading us into a quite unnecessary war.'

Moreover, there was a wide suspicion, voiced eloquently by Tony Benn, but shared by a great many others – that some Ministers saw, in the wake of good Conservative local election results, the bonuses of war for their own political ends: 'A massive task force has been sent. The Prime Minister allows and encourages the idea that a "War Cabinet" meets every day. That is from a Government who say in their document that they have rejected a military policy. The briefings come every day not from the Foreign Office but from the Ministry of Defence. In various speeches the Prime Minister has encouraged what can only be described as war hysteria. I suspect that that is not like the spirit of 1940, but is expressed in a feeling among the people that a military solution is intended, should be supported and will be successful. The world certainly sees it that way, and that is why support for the Government abroad is eroding.'

In addition, there were the immediate reasons of the moment for a vote, put out by a meeting of Frank Allaun, Judith Hart and myself, on the morning of the debate:

'We intend to vote against the Government tonight because: (1) we want to preserve UN negotiations; (2) we demand an immediate ceasefire; (3) we believe military action will serve no purpose in the long run; (4) we want to save British and Argentinian lives.

'We appeal to our fellow MPs to support us.'

11. Dismissal from the Front Bench

So on Thursday, 20 May at 9.59 p.m., one minute before the debate would normally have been adjourned and by prior agreement with Mr Speaker Thomas, I rose in my place to move that 'the Question be now put'—the age-old Parliamentary indication of disagreement on an issue of substance. The whole of the Labour Opposition had been instructed to abstain. Two Welsh Nationalists and thirty-three Labour MPs went into the lobby to vote against the Government, including Andrew Faulds, John Tilley and I, all Front Bench spokesmen. We were left in no doubt that the result of our rebellious action would be dismissal from the Front Bench.

If I dwell on the circumstances of my dismissal as Shadow Spokesman on Science, along with that of Andrew Faulds as Spokesman on Arts and John Tilley as Spokesman on Home Office Affairs, the reader will have to acquit me of egotism. But out dismissal on Monday, 24 May, does encapsulate a number of interrelated problems facing opposition leaderships in general and the official Labour Opposition in relation to the Falklands in particular.

The British system of government is based on the doctrine of collective responsibility. For the system to work, it requires that ministers must adhere to the decisions of their cabinet. It is quite understandable, however, that any man or woman who feels that they are unable to support a firm policy put forward by the reigning administration of which they are a member, must choose between sticking to their beliefs or swallowing their deoubts, between leaving or remaining in the government. On certain issues, such as hanging, there is a free vote, in which MPs can vote according to their consciences: for most decisions the exigencies of power are paramount and policy on the Falklands belonged firmly to this latter category.

The position of dissenters on an opposition front bench, however, is altogether more complex. Their party does not suffer the constraints of wielding power on a day-to-day basis. The coherence of the opposition is an important, but not invariably a paramount consideration. There are no inflexible rules about the required resignation of Front Bench

Opposition Spokesmen for deviating from Shadow Cabinet instructions, of the kind that apply to Ministers currently in office. For example, during consideration of clause 129 of the 1982 Finance Bill, on the politically sensitive topic of alternative valuations of ethane used for petrochemical purposes, five shadow ministers not only failed to vote with the Labour Opposition, but actually went into the Government lobby. Now it might be argued that actually voting with political opponents, as Messrs Donald Dewar, Alex Eadie, Harry Ewing, Martin O'Neill and George Robertson did, was more reprehensible than the action of Dalyell, Faulds and Tilley who voted against the Government, when the official Opposition line was to abstain.

My conclusion is not that Dewar, Eadie, Ewing, O'Neill and Robertson should have been dismissed, as we were. It is rather that in opposition there are situations when it is not unreasonable to defy the principle of collective responsibility and that there should be room for discretion. The question is therefore whether Michael Foot should have exercised discretion and refrained from dismissing us, in view of the fact that dismissal is far from automatic for those who vote in defiance of the Shadow Cabinet.

As we have seen, altogether thirty-three Labour MPs voted against the adjournment of the House at 10 p.m. in the major debate on the Falklands on 20 May. The main purpose of the vote was to demonstrate to the country and to the world that the oft-repeated claim by Government Ministers and others, such as Sir Nicholas Henderson, Ambassador in Washington, that the British Parliament was united behind the sending of the task force, was not true. Thus the vote was not an empty political gesture, but had a specific purpose. Yet we were heavily criticised for our action. *My* criticism of the dissenters is not that we voted on 20 May, but that we failed to do so earlier. The inhibiting factor, of course, was that we were strung along, being told that the success of the peace negotiations was imminent, and that dividing the House would merely show a weakness, thus jeopardising the success of the negotiations. Though we could, and probably ought to have voted on 7th and 29th April and 13th May, when there was an adjournment motion, the fact is that crucially on 3rd April and 14th April they were motions

without vote. This was agreed by the 'usual channels', the
meetings between senior members of government and
opposition, to agree on business. The trouble in this case was
that John Silkin, because he very unusually combined the
roles of Shadow Secretary of State for Defence and Shadow
Leader of the House, was therefore senior Opposition
representative on the 'usual channels'. Being himself less than
keen on a divisive vote, he was only too happy to accept the
Government's proposals for excluding the possibility of a
vote. I am not suggesting a conscious 'fix'. I am suggesting
that the usual parliamentary procedure of excluding the
possibility of a vote on a substantive motion, complicated by
problems of meeting in a recess, suited all participants in the
'usual channel' discussions.

Moreover, I shall always believe that had not the opposition
to the task force become associated in the minds of many
colleagues with what is generically called 'Bennery', there
would have been not thirty-three but sixty or seventy Labour
MPs in the lobby. This had more to do with the internal
problems of the Party than with Tony Benn's speeches on
the Falklands. Both in Hyde Park, where we shared a platform,
and in the House, Tony Benn showed once again that he is
not afraid to say unpopular things. There was nothing in his
speeches to imply that he was jumping on an anti-Fanklands
bandwaggon in the Left of the movement, as has been
suggested. The fact is that Tony Benn was sitting behind me
during the 3 April debate, saying loudly that the Speaker
should call me, very reticent to speak himself, for the
honourable reason that he did not want the Falklands
decision to be involved in his own political persona.

But why, it may be asked, should Michael Foot not have
expected an automatic resignation from me after 20 May,
since I had proffered my resignation on 5 April to the
Opposition Chief Whip? (As we have seen, it was refused
then, at a time when few people thought that the fleet would
have to get much beyond the Western Approaches before
Buenos Aires caved in.) The situation, however, had changed
a great deal since then. In the period between 5 April and
20 May, a substantial amount of support from within the
active branches of the Labour Party had manifested itself
for my viewpoint. Out of sixty-six resolutions received from

constituency parties at the Party headquarters in Walworth Road, no less than sixty were critical of the position adopted by the official Opposition.

In particular, the West Lothian Constituency Labour Party had reiterated its support for my position and the Scottish Trades Union Congress had unanimously passed a resolution opposing the despatch of the task force. Indeed this situation presented something of a microcosm of the deep-seated internal problems of the Labour Party at the present time. Though I have to take responsibility in this instance for being a prime mover, should an MP always give way to the views of the Shadow Cabinet, rather than to those without whose constituency support he would not be an MP? My answer is that every case must be judged on its merits. Sections of the press would have us believe that when MPs take a different line from the Shadow Cabinet they are usually capitulating in craven fashion to pressure from extremists. This is often simply not the situation. A Member of Parliament has a whole range of loyalties, and problems arise when such loyalties conflict. As I see it, I have a loyalty to the Parliamentary Labour Party and its leadership, which is paramount on issues where I do not have more knowledge than most of my colleagues. However, I also owe a strong allegiance to West Lothian Constituency Labour Party, to my sponsoring Trade Union, the National Union of Railwaymen, to the electorate of West Lothian and, ultimately, to my own political beliefs and my family. On the Falklands, some of these loyalties were mutually irreconcilable.

For example, Michael Foot and John Silkin simply did not understand the central conundrum of Defence Policy posed by the Falklands adventure. If we say, 'What we have, we hold' we cannot then prune Defence spending. However, since the Labour Party is in favour of pruning Defence expenditure to the per capita level of our European NATO partners, it is totally inconsistent to think we can adopt this belligerent attitude. One of the main reasons why I voted for Michael Foot rather than Denis Healey in the leadership election of 1980, was that I believed he would authorise the pruning of Defence expenditure as no other Labour leader has felt justified in doing. It is a tragic irony that the Falklands crisis should so badly have dented

Michael Foot's reputation as a life-long peace-monger. Whether Michael Foot, who himself in the 1950s had suffered from authoritarian Labour leaderships in Attlee and Gaitskell days and had had the whip withdrawn, wanted to sack us, I do not know. He denied that it was anyone's decision other than his own, but as an extremely honourable man in such matters he could scarcely say anything else. The fact is that he was under pressure. John Silkin, publicly, and Peter Shore, privately, were among several members of the Shadow Cabinet who lobbied for us to be dismissed for breaking ranks from collective responsibility.

Pressure from Peter Shore I did resent. As a member of the Parliamentary Committee, which meets every Wednesday evening at 5 p.m., he was party to the Shadow Cabinet decisions. This did not inhibit him from appearing on Brian Walden's influential 'Weekend World' television programme and expressing views in favour of hard military action which were as remote from those of most Labour members as mine were from majority Parliamentary Party feeling. With sixty-six votes I myself had had a high vote for the Shadow Cabinet, coming fifth of those who were non-elected and top of those who were neither on a Left- or Right-wing 'slate'. However, I was not a member of the Shadow Cabinet and therefore not formally consulted about their decisions. Peter Shore's attitude was significantly more hawkish than that of the Shadow Foreign Secretary, Denis Healey, who was responsible for the official line of the Shadow Cabinet. Healey said repeatedly that if the use of force on a larger scale became inevitable, then the Opposition would insist that the minimum force be used in order to secure political objectives.

On Saturday, 22 May I wrote to Michael Foot gently suggesting that it was not a good moment for the Party to conduct Shadow bloodletting; if he wanted to reshuffle us out of his team in the Autumn or not to appoint us, if and when he became Prime Minister, he was perfectly entitled to do so. But his mind was made up. Getting rid of Ministers or Shadow Ministers, who are old friends and supporters over many years, is a painful part of the job of any Prime Minister or Opposition Leader. With me, the exchange was wholly civilised and friendly. Michael said he had read my letter

carefully, but pointed out (correctly) that his view on the
Falklands was shared by the majority of the National Executive of the Party. When I suggested that, whereas at the
beginning Party feeling was rather bewildered as to what to
think on the issue, now (by late May) the majority of Party
members shared my general view, Michael commented without
rancour, 'Tam, I think I know as much about the Labour
Party as you do!'

The state of Party feeling could still not be proved one
way or another. However, as we have seen, by the following
week Judith Hart, chairman of the Labour Party, knew that
for the 66 resolutions which had come in to the Walworth
Road headquarters of the Party from the constituencies,
precisely six supported the line of the official Front Bench
and sixty resolutions supported the line of the dissenters. On
the substance of the issue, Michael Foot stood rigidly by
Resolution 502 and the importance of the United Nations.
The trouble with this argument throughout has been that, if
the United Nations was to be the arbiter of paramount
importance, the task force ought to have been sailing under
the UN flag.

In the hour of military victory, Michael Foot offered the
Prime Minister his personal congratulations. This was one of
the saddest moments of my political life. Fundamentally he
had yearned for peace and UN involvement, but had made a
sincere effort to support the Government. For his pains, the
Prime Minister, to borrow James Callaghan's words, 'sneered
across the despatch box' and said that if a Labour Government had been in power, not a shot would have been fired.
While I hope that this is true, it demonstrates how Michael
Foot was strung along, only to be discarded at the end of
the day by an ungrateful and ungracious Prime Minister. One
can only speculate as to what 'Cato', alias Michael Foot, the
author of *Guilty Men* forty years back would have made of
the Greek tragedy of 1982.

Another factor which played an important part in my
dismissal was my appearance on the 'Panorama' television
programme on 12 May, only a week before the debate. The
surrounding furore was the last straw for Michael Foot. In a
sense, voting against the Government on Thursday, 20 May,
was only a logical consequence of my outspoken views,

albeit moderately expressed. I had been approached by the 'Panorama' editor after having repeatedly aired my views about the reluctance of certain service chiefs to embark on a military expedition to the South Atlantic.

Now it is important to understand that there are—and it is healthy that it should be so—different factions within the BBC. One of the strengths of the Corporation is that it is not monolithic. 'Panorama' professed themselves to be unhappy about the fact that the 'dissident voices' had not received a fair hearing from some of their Westminster colleagues, and had it in mind to redress the balance. They therefore decided to interview two Conservative MPs and two Labour MPs who were not of the consensus, followed by Cecil Parkinson, chairman of the Conservative Party, 'to keep the balance'— not that the balance needed keeping, since this programme was screened on Monday, 10 May and on Monday, 3 May, the Prime Minister had had a 'Panorama' programme virtually to herself.

Even the centrepiece of *The Listener* described this 'Panorama' as 'far above the level of intelligence usually shown in the programme. For once it presented the opposition to the Falklands operation in a measured way; these were not strident yobbos with barmy banners, but serious and considerable MPs, sedate and moderate.' The chief interest of the programme, in retrospect, resides in the underlying reasons, as to why it should produce such a violent storm of protest. In the Commons a former Minister of Consumer Affairs, Mrs Sally Oppenheim, was moved to call it 'an odious, subversive travesty', with which the Prime Minister agreed. The popular press fumed, led by *The Sun*, which had capped all else with its notorious headline 'Up your Junta!' The letter columns of *The Times* reverberated with indignation. Mr Robert Kee, presenter of 'Panorama' was moved to write (14 May) 'To follow Mr Tam Dalyell's hearsay assertions that the Chiefs of Staff had been against the task force operations from the start with evidence from an air vice-marshall that they would not have disguised its realities (as if this were somehow confirmation of the hearsay) seemed to me poor objective journalism, as did several other aspects of the film' (for a transcript of what the author actually said, see Appendix D). Kee went on to complain that my charge against Mrs

Thatcher of 'war-mongering' went unrefuted. A powerful letter
from Michael Cockerell, who interviewed me on 'Panorama'
raised the obvious point that even if the opinion polls indicated
80 : 20 in favour of the Government's action, the one in five
majority were entitled to have their views heard.

It was this last consideration that was an important ingredient
of the storm which followed the 'Panorama' of the dissenters, or
dissidents, as we came to be tagged. The media are naturally
exceedingly interested in protecting their own freedoms. The
very idea that 'Panorama' should not invite David Crouch, Tory
MP for Canterbury, George Foulkes, Labour MP for South Ayrshire, Anthony Meyer, Tory MP for Flint, and myself onto their
programme, because we disagreed with the consensus was a
matter which interested every journalist in the land. As Colin
Mackay, presenter of Scottish Television's programme, 'Ways
and Means', put it to me after the 'Panorama' row had blown
up: 'We must have you on our programme this week, to show
that the Independent Television companies are shoulder to
shoulder with the BBC on this issue.' A further rare occurrence
was the appearance of George Howard, chairman of the Board
of Governors of the BBC, on the 'Today' programme, defending the actions of his younger producers in allowing the
dissenters to put their view.

What really irked many vocal supporters of the task force
about the 'Panorama' programme was the spectacle of four
apparently moderate, sensible, Members of Parliament putting
a rational case in a gentle but firm way, on the recognised
flagship programme of BBC television. I believe that the case
against sending the task force had been greatly damaged by
being associated with extremism of one kind and another.
Visual images of extreme groups carrying banners, calling for
an Argentinian victory, were immeasurably damaging to the
case of those who opposed the war and a positive gift to the
popular press who were 'backing our boys'. Another raw
nerve which this interview touched upon was the realisation
for the first time that Britain could be heading for a military
catastrophe of major proportions. One of the curious aspects
of the attitude in Britain throughout April was the assumption
that we would not have to fight, but that if we were obliged
to fight, it would be a walk-over. Such notions were to be
rudely shattered in early May.

12. *The Cost*

The day after that critical debate of 20 May, more than 5,000 British marines and soldiers established a bridgehead at Port San Carlos on East Falkland. HMS *Ardent* was sunk by air attack in Falkland Sound. Two days later the Argentinian airforce returned, sinking HMS *Antelope*; in a period of three days the Argentinians lost 25 aircraft. On 25 May, Argentine's national day, HMS *Coventry* was sunk and the *Atlantic Conveyor* abandoned after being struck by an Exocet missile. The Parachute Regiment took Goose Green and Darwin on 27 May and by the end of the month British troops were overlooking Port Stanley, which finally fell on 15 June.

The British position in the Falklands constitutes an indefinite problem of growing dimensions. Any idea that a token garrison will suffice to defend the islands is unrealistic. All the signs show that the Argentinians are determined to modernise their forces, precisely along the clear lines which General Nicolaides, General Galtieri's successor as Army Commander, outlined at the beginning of July. Moreover, this attitude is not only to be found amongst the most senior officers of the Argentine forces. The parting words of the local officer in charge at Uschaia to the British journalists, Ian Mather and Simon Winchester, were that his countrymen would return to the Malvinas. They will accumulate such modern weapons as they can afford, with as much speed as they can muster, to achieve that end.

The first cost of the Falklands adventure has been in blood. Two hundred and fifty-five young British lives were lost; more than 770 were maimed and will carry awful scars of mind and body until the end of their days. Today's heroes will tend to be tomorrow's forgotten passengers of society. In my constituency work I sometimes visit war-blinded of World War II, whose wounds were inflicted in actions no less gallant and no less dramatic than those at Goose Green. How many now really care about what happened in those far-off days of the 1940s? Even their relatives have too often distanced themselves from the war-wounded, regarding them as a burden on their own lives. So, doubtless, in the course of

time will be the fate of those who were flown in on
stretchers to RAF Brize Norton.

The official figure for Argentine casualties has not, at the
time of writing, been disclosed, but Buenos Aires has
suggested a figure of 712 killed. Probably it exceeds the British
figures by a factor of four or five. Once blood is spilled on
such a scale, for a nation as deeply concerned with *macho*
and pride as the Argentinians, mending fences becomes very
difficult. Did they all die in vain? That will be the refrain for
generations to come in Argentina.

The cost to Argentina in terms of resources has been the
resultant chaos in the economy. With debts some four times
as large as those of Poland, Argentina is one of the major
borrowers of the Western world. Long-term defaulting by
Argentina would cause trouble, not only in Latin America,
but throughout the banking system of the West. This was a
point which was well understood by Lloyds' Bank in London,
the Bank of London and South America, and merchant banks
such as Baring Brothers who specialise in South American
investment Though they made their disquiet known throughout the Falklands crisis, and though a number of leaders of
commerce such as Lord Montgomery did voice their misgivings, their criticism of British Government policy was
remarkable for its restraint. The truth is that, in the face of
the euphoria generated by the task force, the City of London
did not want to be deemed unpatriotic. Since their criticism
was so muted, little heed was paid to them. Having lunched
at Lloyds' Insurance in late May, I can understand that
dissident voices in the City at that time would have received
short shrift from most of those who were abysmally ignorant
about South America. It is doubtful whether the actual and
potential loss of trade in South America generally, for
Britain, can ever be quantified. The hostility which erupted
at Caracas Airport in far away Venezuela, when staff refused
to handle British Caledonian planes, is just an example of
the strength of feeling generated against Britain by the task
force.

As to the actual cost, there are, first, the official figures.
Defence Secretary Nott told the Commons on 5 July 1982
that £500 million was the preliminary estimate of both the
equipment and the operational running costs in the financial

year 1982/83 of the Falkland Islands Campaign. This included an amount for replacing lost equipment, although a proportion of the total equipment replacement costs arising from the campaign would fall in 1983/84 and subsequent years. It was too early to say, claimed the Defence Secretary, what would be the cost per year of maintaining forces in and around the Falklands from the time when Argentinian forces surrendered.

So much for the official Government estimates. The truth is that, from early April, a succession of Government estimates of cost have been ludicrously optimistic. First, the explanation was that the costs of the task force could 'be lost' in the £2.4 billion Contingency Fund which every British Government carries. The additional, marginal costs of maintaining the task force, over and above the regular costs of maintaining forces, were said to be nugatory. But those estimates belonged to the heady days before losses of men and material were publicly contemplated. As at the end of September 1982, the estimated cost of the campaign had soared to £1,600 million, excluding the recurring annual burden of garrisoning the islands and providing lines of communication. Some measure of the enormity of these costs is provided by one statistic which we do know: the cost of one Hercules giant transport plane flying the round trip from Britain to the Falklands, in fuel and landing costs, is £¾ million. *The Observer* for 19 September reported that official papers circulating in Whitehall indicated that the escalating costs of defending the islands was threatening to to cause further reductions in spending on education and social services at home next year. The Shackleton Report (1982) recommend spending on civilian projects totalling £75 million, but it was understood that the capital costs of defending the Falklands was projected at between £250 and £500 million in the 1982/83 financial year. These figures do not include the running costs of supporting Britain's military commitment there. The Government was reported, in the same *Observer* article, as seeking to purchase at least four new Phantom aircraft at a cost of nearly £100 million; other capital expenses will be for a new airfield, which could cost between £30 and £50 million, and for a Rapier low-level, anti-aircraft system.

There are other less quantifiable costs to be reckoned resulting from the damage done to the Anglo-American relationship. Who can suppose, for instance,.that the harshness of the American attitude on European American-owned industries' participation in the Soviet gas pipeline project was unrelated to the coolness engendered in the Anglo-American relationship by the Falklands crisis.

The cost in equipment alone has been astronomical. Forty-six merchant ships were requisitioned, at an initial cost of £40 million, and subsequently, according to Lloyds Insurance, at a cost of £30 million per month. Warship replacement of the two Type 42 and two Type 21 frigate/destroyer ships of the Sheffield and Coventry classes would exceed £1 billion. Even the *Atlantic Conveyor* was credited with a replacement value of £20 million, a substantial sum for an elderly cargo vessel. A 'Tigerfish' torpedo costs a cool £½ million; a sea-dart missile £60,000, the invaluable side-winder missile, £30,000, the Rapier, £25,000, and even the humble 30 mm bullet, £2 each, fired, *in extremis*, at more than 1,000 rounds per minute.

When the cheering dies down, bills for all this and much more will have to be paid. Yet, during the campaign, the question of costs was swept under the carpet of patriotism. As early as 8 April, William Hamilton MP asked Mrs Thatcher, 'Does the Prime Minister agree with the statement made by the Secretary of State for Defence yesterday that the Falkland Islands exercise will go ahead, regardless of cost? Has she any idea of what that cost will be — £100 million, £500 million, £1,000 million? How will it be paid for, and how does it come within the cash limits of the Ministry of Defence?'

The Prime Minister replied: 'I wish to make it perfectly clear to the hon. Gentleman that when this information first came to me — I said when it did — I took a decision immediately and said that the future of freedom and the reputation of Britain were at stake. We cannot therefore look at it on the basis of precisely how much it will cost. That is what the Contingency Reserve is for. I understand that my right hon. and learned Friend the Chancellor of the Exchequer has said that, should we need to raise more money, that money will be raised in orthodox ways, and that it will not be done in an inflationary way.'

The replacement of 7 ships and 19 aircraft may turn out to be a lesser problem than the expensive changes in defence strategy which may ensue as the result of a policy geared to defend the Falklands for the foreseeable future, against the prospect of ever more sophisticated weaponry. The Falklands are a unique, one-off, end-of-empire commitment and therefore costly in the way that all one-off products are costly. The requirement for the defence of the Falklands is unlikely to be repeated in any other geographical and military context. There can rarely, if ever, have been such an example of a tail, in the shape of 1,800 people, 'wagging the dog' of the defence strategy of more than 50 million people. High-sounding principles are all very well, but the crude calculation is that by the end of June 1982, more than £1 million per head per Falklander had been spent. This kind of money is forthcoming from British governments for one imperative cause – that of saving the political face of the most senior ministers. The upholding of elevated moral principles would not have been a sufficient spur to force the Treasury to disgorge such colossal sums of money.

The refusal of the Argentine Government to declare an end to hostilities, and the uncertainty which would perforce surround any pledge by any Argentine government to suspend hostilities in the absence of agreement about the sovereignty of the Malvinas, creates a gloomy outlook for the British tax-payer. Dr Paul Rogers of the Bradford University School of Peace Studies suggests that should the Argentine Government present a convincing threat of low-intensity operations, the annual bill could amount to £600 million at 1982 prices. Dr Rogers's work is based on tables published in the 1981 Defence White Paper. As the Argentine threat persists, it will be necessary to develop Port Stanley as a South Atlantic Naval Base with repair facilities for a frigate and destroyer force. The Royal Air Force will certainly require a base with hangars and workshops. The Army will need barracks for a garrison of brigade size around Port Stanley, with lesser garrisons at Goose Green, Pebble Island and Fox Bay in West Falkland. Troop movements will necessitate the construction of 200 miles of road in exceedingly difficult terrain. Water supplies and sewage disposal will have to be arranged and a hospital developed. The whole complex will require a ground air defence system with radar, guns and missiles. A supply train from Britain will need to be maintained by sea and by air. The forces will need to use the American facility of Ascension Island, for ships and aircraft on the way to and from Port Stanley. This, in turn, will demand more British forces remaining at Ascension. All this adds up, at the very least, to a situation where 1,800 Falkland islanders are being protected on a 4:1 ratio by over 7,000 British service personnel.

It has been argued that some of these resources needed in the Falklands, should be found from the existing British contribution to NATO in the North Atlantic. Now, I was struck forcefully by the fact that throughout April, May and June 1982 NATO seemed to be more unworried than I would have expected, by the British preoccupation in the South Atlantic. I regretted this relaxed attitude, since NATO objection was one of the few pressures that might have halted the Prime Minister in her tracks. The truth was, it seemed to me as the task force sailed south, that NATO leaders viewed it as a short-term diversion which would be a nine weeks' wonder. However, I learned from two chance meetings with NATO officers of non-British nationality, that they were intrigued and professionally fascinated to learn how modern missiles would actually perform in a wartime situation. After all, there had never been a missile war involving surface ships and missiles, and naval exercises, however seriously carried out, are no substitute for the actuality of war. Now that the Falklands have been retaken, our NATO partners are beginning to insist that the full British commitment in the North Atlantic should be honoured. So the facile debating-point that the cost of permanent commitment to garrisoning the Falklands can be somehow gouged out of our existing defence funds, is a hollow sham. On the contrary, General Sir John Hackett, former Commander of NATO's Northern Army Group, could contribute a centre-page article to *The Sunday Times* of 20 June, 'More, Much More, for Defence'. And James Callaghan, speaking in the Defence debate of 6 July in the House, could forget his years as a harassed Chancellor of the Exchequer and call for a much enlarged Navy, provoking even Defence Secretary Nott to interrupt him to ask where the resources were coming from.

One of the unexplained, and possibly inexplicable, features of the spring of 1982 was the seeming reluctance of public opinion to make the connection between the cost of the expedition to the South Atlantic and the economic catastrophe at home. Perhaps they were drugged into quiescence by the mesmeric Falklands Extra on Independent Television 'News at Ten' each night? For example, on Wednesday, 16 June, I went to Bridlington in Yorkshire to give a lunch-time fringe speech on the Falklands to the annual conference of the Confederation of Health Service Employees. A good audience said to me that on account of the Falklands, they were unable to focus public attention on urgent questions of stoppages in hospitals, nurses' pay and strike action by woefully underpaid hospital ancillary employees. Equally urgent decisions about the future of the railways in Britain were put off repeatedly. As one Permanent Secretary confided to me, it was just not possible to get the concentration of senior Ministers on matters other than the South Atlantic. As far as reaching decisions on other matters was concerned, Whitehall virtually seized up.

Hence the question that was insufficiently asked throughout the time that British servicemen were in the field: 'Exactly what priority is to be accorded to the issues in the South Atlantic? Is it more important that Britain maintains her position in the Falkland Islands than that finance be found to send 40,000 of our qualified young people, who five years ago would certainly have gained university entrance to degree courses?' (On the very day that the Prime Minister told the House that no one could put a price tag on freedom for the Falklanders, the University of Glasgow found itself in so parlous a financial condition that it was obliged to put some of its ancient treasures on the market.) Does the allocation of resources to the Falklands really come before funds to keep open training centres run by the Industrial Training Boards on which our future as an industrial nation depends? The proverbial one-hundred-and-one deserving domestic causes could be enumerated. Yet in early April interrogation of Ministers in Parliament, as to the priority of funds for the Falklands over their own cherished Departmental programmes, proved fruitless. Moreover, in the British system of government departmental Ministers are dependent on, and

usually in awe of, the Prime Minister who can dispense
patronage: they are not going to fight on matters which they
know are jealously preserved by the political stratosphere. I
first learned this truth when, as Richard Crossman's Parliamentary Private Secretary, I voiced controversial views against
British participation in the Borneo War and Indonesian
Confrontation. I was told sternly by Crossman that not even
he, as a Cabinet Minister, meddled in the highly sensitive
areas of East of Suez. So, in 1967, I resigned from being
Crossman's PPS, in order not to embarrass his relations with
Harold Wilson — and was brought back nine months later by
Crossman, since I was useful to him.

One of the lessons to be learnt from this unwillingness to
discuss cost priorities in relation to the Falklands, is that it
is intolerable that decisions, of which the consequences will
rumble on through British industry, commerce and politics
for years to come — are taken by so few people. Whose fault
is it? In the first place, it is the fault of any Cabinet Minister
or Minister who disapproves of the policy for not standing
up and being counted. Secondly, it is the fault of Members
of the House of Commons, collectively, for allowing themselves to be trampled on.

It is fashionable for political commentators to shake their
heads and lament — often with more than a touch of *schaden-
freude* — the internal wranglings between the Labour Party in
the country and the Parliamentary Labour Party. Yet, here
we have a specific example of what much of, though not all,
the Party trouble is about. Without fear of contradiction, I
assert that rightly or wrongly a decisive majority of Labour
Party activists would not have given defence of the Falklands,
after the Argentine invasion, priority over financing the Health
Service, schools, investment in railways or sewers. But, unasked,
the Labour leadership meekly fell in behind Mrs Thatcher in
her war. No consultation occurred with the Party in the
country. Nor will it do to respond to Labour activists that
there was no time for such consultation. A holding reply, at
least, could have been given on 3 April, to allow for consultation. This need not have been interpreted as weakness or
indecisiveness. It seems likely that leaders are pressured by
the media to make swift decisions. But one of the yardsticks
of sound leadership, surely, is the strength to resist being

goaded or jostled into positions about which one is subsequently unhappy.

There was, however, a matter which was giving even more concern in the grassroots of the Labour Party than defending the Falkland islanders. This was the subject of arms sales, the topic of countless resolutions at Party Conferences during the past two decades, and it is to this aspect that we must now turn.

13. Now Thrive the Armourers

Just as the NATO commanders in the North Atlantic could scarcely contain their curiosity in learning how sophisticated missiles worked in real battle, so there was another group who were not a whit less interested: the arms manufacturers themselves.

Though no Minister would admit it, I am forced to the conclusion that some politicians were far from unhappy at the prospect of hot fighting. Their feelings were that, in a containable situation, it would give servicemen who had had no training in real battle conditions, something of a 'dry-run' and would at the same time enable us to ascertain the capabilities of modern weaponry.

Not that it was a matter of cold calculation from 2 April. The truth, as usual, is blurred. The only certainty is that when leaders of nations go to war for what is, or is stated to be, a principle, the final result may be very different from what they either wanted in the first place or believed to be a likely outcome. Let us, therefore, say in charity that, given the events in the South Atlantic, there was presented an opportunity for men and weapons to be tested in a war situation without threat of a holocaust. No less important, conditions were created where life-support systems for the forces and logistics could be tested. From 2 May, with the sinking of the *Belgrano* and the retaliatory sinking of HMS *Sheffield*, arms manufacturers, French makers of Exocet no less than British makers of Harriers, were busy putting the 'Falklands-tested tag' onto their wares. A boost was given to industry in many fields of the defence manufacturing industry, such as electro-optics.

Better still from the point of view of the armaments industry, there is provided by war a case for a perceived need, of which governments might not previously have been aware. Let us pursue the particular case of the electro-optics industry, for the purposes of example. In the middle of May it became part of the currency of Ministerial broadcasts that we were fighting to 'defend the sea lanes round Cape Horn'. But the big oil tankers ploughing their way to and from Alaska had been perfectly safe, until we started the war. No opportunity, however, was lost by makers of armaments in the electro-optics field in suggesting that the hitherto unthreatened tankers ought to have the most sophisticated electro-optical equipment with which to defend themselves against potential attack. Shakespeare had a phrase for it: 'Now thrive the armourers'. The eagerness evinced at the arms sale showpiece at Aldershot by British arms manufacturers to sell round the world can only fuel the suspicion that our motives in going to war were not quite as pure as they had been made out to be.

By the middle of May, a cacophony of pertinent questions was being asked by a few people. Was Britain prepared to restructure the fleet, in such a way as to keep a proportion of it 8,000 miles away? Why was the Royal Navy task force sent south without adequate air-cover? (This, as we have seen, was not a matter of hindsight.) Was it thought that the original Harriers packed into the *Invincible* and the *Hermes* were sufficient to maintain standing patrols and prevent Exocet-carrying Etandard planes approaching close enough for a lethal strike against HMS *Sheffield*? Why was there no air-borne radar surveillance? Why were Sea Wolf missiles, which are the most effective available counter to Exocet, not in place on the task force destroyers? Was was the destroyer which had to be placed on radar piquet patrol (*Antelope*), so shamefully under-equipped to protect itself from missile strike? (Similar Soviet destroyers positively bristle with defensive weaponry and *Sheffield* was naked by comparison.) What was it about the materials used in the construction of the British warships which enabled one missile hit to turn the ship into a blazing inferno which had to be abandoned? Are other fighting ships as fire-vulnerable as HMS *Sheffield*? If so, what would have happened if the Super-Etandard had received the promised wing-tanks from the United States, embargoed at the last moment at the airport? With its range extended it could have penetrated with air-launched Exocet the defensive screen and found its way into a carrier's hangar deck full of Harriers and fuel. How was it that a significant number of deaths occurred from fumes given off by melting insulating materials covering the miles of cabling found in any modern warship?

All these questions and more were asked both inside and

outside the House of Commons. In the middle of hostilities, of course, Ministers had the heaven-sent excuse that it was not appropriate to answer them. Indeed, the implication was that it was disloyal and unpatriotic even to pose them at such a stressful time. But it was not only Ministers and their supporters who put pressure on the dissenting voices to remain silent during the hostilities. Some Labour colleagues were virulent in their condemnation of those who challenged the continuation of the war on the ground that it could become – as it so easily might have done – a military calamity of the first order for Britain. I had Captain Roskill, the famous naval historian quoted at me, 'I doubt whether in the long history of the navy, it has ever been given a more difficult job' than the Falklands. I was particularly conscious of the severe displeasure of my former Prime Minister, James Callaghan. Like others, he took the view that the Labour Party had 'lost out' by being thought unpatriotic during the Suez crisis and that if there were to be another Labour government, we would be expected by the British 'people' to be 'responsible' and not let the forces down, right or wrong. I believed that our obligation to the fighting men was not our automatic support, but our best Judgement; if that judgement suggested the real possibility of appalling loss of life – which would have been the case if one of the carriers or a troopship had been badly hit – we, as democratically elected representatives, had a duty to say so. In fact, as we later learnt, if all the Argentinian bombs that reached their targets had detonated, the loss of ships, men and equipment would have been catastrophic.

For the Air Force strategists, the questions were hardly less acute. Was it safe to rely on dog-fighting aircraft like the Harrier, when the stand-off success of the Super Etandard suggested that there was little occasion for classic air dog-fights? Has not stand-off weaponry, coupled with improved communications and intensely accurate targeting transformed the practice of modern warfare? Was not the sinking of the *Sheffield* a turning-point in 5,000 years of naval history, in that never again could a capital surface ship be deemed relatively safe and protected from air-launched, surface-skimming missiles? It was because I asked informed questions of this nature that I became involved in the controversy I

have already mentioned – 'The Unpatriotic 'Panorama' Crisis',
as it came to be called.

As I have indicated in Chapter 3, 'The Military', prompted
by my talks with Arthur Tedder, I challenged Ministers as
early as 7 April, face to face, on the professional advice they
had been given. At the beginning of May, the Commander-in-
Chief, Admiral Sir John Fieldhouse, was interviewed at press
conferences and on television. He kept using the phrase
'within our capability' to describe his assessment of the
likelihood of the success of the operation to retake the
Falkland Islands. Meanwhile, I had been given to understand,
as I have shown, that members of the Air Staff, deeply
anxious that they should not be plamed for the lack of air
cover being provided for British ships, wanted it to be known
that they had indeed advised against the sending of a task
force to an area in which it could not be given air cover, from
land-based planes. The Air Advisers pointed out that the
shape of our forces was geared to the specific requirements
of NATO in the North Atlantic and Europe, where the RAF
were structured to give protection to ships. If Ministers and
politicians wanted to send expeditions to the Falklands,
against an opponent with a modern, well-equipped Air Force,
the whole British defence capability would have to be
restructured.

14. The Role of the Iron Lady

There could be interminable argument about whether the wishes of the Falkland islanders were to be 'paramount': there can be no argument at all that the character of the British Prime Minister was a 'paramount' factor in the British reaction. Once it had become apparent that there was anger and consternation among the British press and public following the Argentinian military occupation, Mrs Thatcher's demeanour became increasingly aggressive and bellicose. A Prime Minister's demeanour in a crisis can itself become an important factor. She decided to be decisive at all times and therefore became inflexible.

At this point, I hazard two guesses, which by their very nature cannot be proved or disproved. My first guess is that, from Friday, 2 April, Mrs Thatcher was haunted by the tales of chronic indecision which pervaded her Downing Street house almost exactly a quarter of a century before. Lady Eden had been moved to remark that she thought the Suez Canal was flowing through her dining-room. (Unlike Sir Anthony Eden in 1956, at the time of the crisis with Col. Nasser, Mrs Thatcher enjoys rude good health and displays an astonishing stamina, that even her critics have to admire.) It is not uncommon for political leaders to over-react to what they see as the mistakes of their predecessors in seemingly parallel situations, or to draw misleading conclusions.

My second guess is that Mrs Thatcher has come to glory in the nickname of the 'Iron Lady'. Like many other leaders in the past, she may well feel that she has to live up to her image. Iron Ladies cannot afford to dither and prevaricate: the ability to make up one's mind and act promptly and decisively is all part of the business of being an Iron Lady. Flexibility is not one of the ingredients of being an Iron Lady. I believe that much of what occurred in April and in the weeks that followed, stemmed from the spectre of Eden, and the Prime Minister's self-image. But first of all, I feel it incumbent on me to be fair to the Prime Minister on a number of matters before April 1982, and some after April 1982, on which the great majority of her other critics and opponents have harped.

It would be humbug and hypocrisy for me, of all people, to cast blame on Mrs Thatcher for not having a permanent sizeable military force garrisoned in the Falklands to deter Argentinian action. Firstly, I would have argued that the presence of such a force was, in itself, a provocation to Latin Americans and an impediment to our prime interest of good relations with Latin America. Secondly, I would have argued that if money could have been spent on a garrison, the £12 million that the Shackleton Committee wanted for civilian infrastructure purposes had a higher priority. Thirdly, if I had known that there were conflicts in Cabinet and Cabinet sub-committees, in which the Prime Minister threw her weight behind not sending nuclear-powered submarines to the South Atlantic in order to restrain Ministry of Defence spending, I should have had to agree with her.

If later, I offer harsh criticism of the Prime Minister, it is not on account of her original attitudes to the Falklands and their defence, but because she adopted a line totally inconsistent with these beliefs and careered off in other directions (see Appendix A).

However, there is one point at which I would criticise Mrs Thatcher's defence strategy prior to the crisis. The announcement that the 25-year-old ice patrol ship, HMS *Endurance*, should be withdrawn from duty in the South Atlantic was, in my opinion, a blunder. With her two Wasp light helicopters and two 20mm guns, *Endurance* could not have mounted significant resistance to a determined force. However, psychologically, news of her withdrawal was another signal which Buenos Aires could interpret as British willingness to relinquish relinquish responsibility for the Falklands.

However, I do not believe, as many have claimed, that Mrs Thatcher did not care. The lady I saw in her room on 21 April was worried sick about what might happen to many young Britons in the task force. My judgement was that she was genuinely appalled. And any MP who observed her at close quarters on that dreadful night of 4 May, sitting dressed in black beside Defence Secretary John Nott while he told us that HMS *Sheffield* had been sunk with losses, must have sensed that there was a genuinely distressed soul. Whether she was distressed about the loss of life or potential military defeat I shall never know. My instinct tells me that Mrs

Thatcher was, in her private moments more deeply touched
by the deaths, burns and maiming than she felt it prudent
publicly to reveal.

The complaint about Mrs Thatcher relates not to her private
persona, but rather to her public actions as Prime Minister
and her general warlike demeanour.

The first charge is that a combination of injured political
pride and domestic political considerations, interacting with
one another, propelled her into hasty decisions. In particular,
she was confronted with the outraged gut reaction of those
back-benchers and those sections of the press who had made
her Leader of the Conservative Party against all the odds in
the first place. She must have realised that her own political
skin was in grave danger. Certainly after, if not before, Monday,
5 April, when Lord Carrington fell on his political sword and
insisted on resigning, her survival as head of the Government
was in the forefront of her mind. In practical terms, this
called for immediate action. She never gave any sign of
stopping to think of how, when she had opened Pandora's
Box, she would close it: how, once having decided to send an
armada, she would bring it back from half-way round the
world without fighting in earnest? It would have been in the
character of all her immediate predecessors as Prime Minister,
including Eden, to have played for time — to have gone to the
United Nations properly; to have consulted the United States
in depth; even to have talked directly to the Argentinians,
before embarking on so enormous and so predictably
consequential an enterprise as the task force. All her post-
war predecessors have hankered after consensus, Parliamentary and national. If Mrs Thatcher thought that she had
snatched apparent Parliamentary consensus, she must have
known that outside Parliament, not least in the Foreign
Office, there was no consensus for sending gunboats. Being
against the consensus is for her a virtue in itself, and an added
virtue if the leader of consensus opinion happens to be the
Foreign Office, whose officials are to her as the red rag is to
a bull. (The feeling of distaste is unconcealed and reciprocated.)

The second and related charge against her is that she
resolutely declined to give her mind to the long-term consequences of her actions. The task force sailed because *something had to be done*. As to clear objectives, there were none.

Policy was made up as we went along. For example, on BBC 'Panorama' on Monday, 3 May, she blurted out a so-called plan for the permanent stationing of troops from a number of nations to garrison the Falklands more or less in perpetuity, without even consulting the Americans. They, naturally, already dismayed at bitching their own long-term relations with South America, would not entertain such a scheme. This episode reveals the Prime Minister's penchant for instant policy-making without consulting those who would be directly and obviously involved. It is by no means an isolated instance. On 14 February 1980, Mrs Thatcher announced to the House of Commons that the Government thought that the British Olympic Team should not attend the Moscow Games, without even mentioning the subject to Sir Denis Followes, the chairman of the British Olympic Committee. Never, in the House of Commons, would she address her mind to the problems and perils of supplying the Falkland Islands from Britain on a scale much enhanced by the presence of a sizeable garrison; of providing protection for ships or covoys going to the Islands; of the British community in Argentina, in the event of a hostile reaction to defeat in Argentina; or of our future interests throughout the Hispanic world.

During the whole crisis, Mrs Thatcher lacked the steadying influence of the Foreign Office, which in previous crises, such as Rhodesia, had brought her to reason or saved her from impetuous folly. She makes no attempt to hide her disdain for the Foreign Office officials and prefers to operate through the Cabinet Office. Her lack of any clear purpose beyond recapturing the Falklands and inflicting the revenge of unconditional surrender on Argentina alarmed the Americans and our European partners, and could never have had the approval of experienced Foreign Office men, who will have to live in the international world long after Mrs Thatcher has passed from the scene. I myself questioned Francis Pym on the role of the Foreign Office during the crisis.

The House, when it heard the exchange, simply gave one of those collective laughs, which indicate that everybody knows that what a questioner says is true and that the Minister who has to answer accepts the justice of the question: 'Who runs British foreign policy?' I asked. 'Is it the Foreign Office and the much-maligned Foreign Office civil servants or

is it Downing Street? Has the Foreign Secretary seen that the
political editor of *The Times* has outlined in detail on the
front page the very real rift that seems to exist between
Downing Street and the Foreign Office and that Peter Jenkins
in *The Guardian* talks of a diplomatic rump in Downing
Street? Are these reports completely without foundation?'

Playing his own politics, the Foreign Secretary replied
ruefully: 'Whatever the answer to that question, I am sure
that the hon. Gentleman does not run British foreign policy.
I would not comment upon highly speculative pieces in the
newspapers that are written from time to time for one reason
or another. The answer is that my right hon. Friend the Prime
Minister charged me with responsibility for British foreign
policy, for better or for worse. I do my best to fulfil that
responsibility.'

The German general and writer on war, Karl von Clause-
witz, allocated hatred as the response of the *people* in time
of hostilities, and prudence and restraint as the appropriate
qualities of their *leaders*. In the Falklands conflict there was
very little popular passion for the war as such, in contrast
to the genuine admiration felt for the brave soldiers, sailors,
marines and airmen; people, however they wanted to 'back
our boys', did not hate the Argentinians. There was too
little prudence from the Prime Minister and this the Foreign
Office well knew, and let it be known that they knew,
which made Mrs Thatcher resent them all the more.

Mrs Thatcher has never wanted to understand the argument
that in the long term the Argentinians will always believe
that the Malvinas are an integral part of their country, whatever the complexion of the government in Buenos Aires.
This awkward truth was encapsulated by Foreign Minister
Aguirrie Lanari, on 12 July, when he declared: 'Peace will be
precarious while there is colonial rule.' The Prime Minister's
cardinal weakness is that she is constitutionally unable to
put herself in other people's shoes.

My third charge against the Prime Minister is that, having
obtained the support—such as it was—of the official
Opposition, she accorded too much weight to the needs of
the Conservative Party. It was no accident that Mrs Thatcher
brought in her henchman, the chairman of the Tory Party,
Cecil Parkinson, to be a member of the inner War Cabinet.

His presence provided her with an inbuilt 3 to 2 majority, over the Home Secretary and Deputy Prime Minister William Whitelaw and the Foreign Secretary Francis Pym. I believe that at various stages Whitelaw and Pym would have settled for a compromise peace: Mrs Thatcher outmanoeuvred them. However, it has to be said that if they had been determined and presented her with a joint resignation, her position would have been pitifully weak. As Lady Bracknell might have said, to lose one Foreign Secretary in a major crisis, may be regarded as a misfortune; to lose a second one and a Home Secretary is not sustainable in terms of a Prime Minister's political survival.

To suggest that Mrs Thatcher was simply a pawn in the hands of her backbenchers would be altogether too crude an assessment of the relationship. Certainly she tends to divide her Parliamentary colleagues into two categories – 'one of us' or 'one of them' – friends and critics. It was her friends who were most strident in their call for action, of course, and her critics who were cautious. In the knowledge that she had become leader of the Tory Party because Edward Heath had not sufficiently cultivated *his* friends when he was Party leader, Mrs Thatcher has always made strenuous efforts to cultivate *her* friends. While she is autocratic in her Cabinet and with Ministers who are not in her Cabinet, she is assiduous in keeping in step with her backbench friends: if things had gone wrong, militarily, she would have needed them.

The fourth and last charge against her is altogether of a graver nature: that she got herself into a frame of mind where she actually looked forward to a fight. To the dismay of experienced Foreign Office officials and others with Latin American experience, she refused to contemplate the consequences for Britain of winning the battle for the Falklands. Military victory was an end in itself. Nothing else mattered. When the former NATO commander, Secretary of State Alexander Haig, said that there could be no military solution in the Falklands, Mrs Thatcher was undeterred. Her demeanour was that of a politician who, whatever the price, whatever the consequences, is determined to win. She spurned a negotiated peace settlement. Had it been otherwise, her Government would have accepted the proposals from Peru at the beginning of May. As I have shown, when an honourable peace was within her grasp, Mrs Thatcher chose to scupper it. Nor is it only the sinking of the *Belgrano* and the circumstances surrounding that act that lead an objective observer to the conclusion that Mrs Thatcher was escalating hostilities whenever a mediation plan showed promise of success. The extension of the exclusion zone to 12 miles off the Argentine coast on 7 May, coincided with one of the hopeful 'ups' in the several ups and downs of the UN peace attempts. Another episode, the capture of the Argentinian fishing vessel *Narwal* on 9 May and its sinking the next day followed immediately on another 'up' on the roller coaster at the UN. If the timing was chance, it was clumsy to the point of being criminal. These incidents were almost certainly the carefully orchestrated actions of a British Prime Minister, the main purpose of whose 'peace efforts' was to demonstrate to the British people that there was no alternative to war. Any leader genuinely in search of peace, would have made sure that such incidents were not allowed to occur at crucial moments in negotiation.

Throughout the conflict, it seemed to me that Mrs Thatcher, publicly and privately, associated peace with surrender. Military victory, *per se*, was what her Britain really needed, as a national therapy. And, into the bargain, it would prove that she was a 'better man, than the men around her'. At the highest level in politics, trifling considerations of a personal nature can become very important indeed in the minds of leaders. Deep down in herself, I suspected from her parliamentary appearances, she took a wry, perverse pleasure in being tougher and more martial than those around her — Carrington, Whitelaw and Pym — all of whom had had a 'good war' in 1939-45. At times during the conflict, she was frighteningly exhilarated by what she saw as the Falklands' challenge. Indeed, following her triumphant appearance at the Scottish Conservative Party Conference in May, she let slip to an interviewer on Radio Clyde that she had found dealing with what she regarded as the great issues of principle and right and wrong of the Falklands crisis, as much more interesting than the everyday topics of social services and economics, the stuff politicians normally had to concern themselves with.

The events of early May confirmed my suspicions of April,

that what really worried the Prime Minister was that Al
Haig's shuttle diplomacy between London and Buenos Aires
would come up with an offer she would find it difficult to
persuade her backbenchers in the House to accept. Possibly
too slowly, it had dawned on critics of sending the task force,
that Mrs Thatcher was not allowing any concessions from
Britain which could help Haig in his negotiations in Buenos
Aires. If Britain had allowed Haig to talk in terms of a brief
resumption of administration and a negotiated transfer of
sovereignty, he might have had more success. In the event,
he went to Buenos Aires empty-handed. Had Mrs Thatcher
been so minded, she could have made concessions which
would have created the conditions for a peaceful solution.
Sources close to President Reagan were quoted as saying
'That lady wants a war.' As time went on even the charitable
could offer no other interpretation of her demeanour and
handling of the crisis.

Indeed, the only success Haig did have was to restrain Mrs
Thatcher from the folly of ordering the bombing of the
South American mainland. The operational reasons for so
doing were far from negligible: for with surface ships
vulnerable to land-based aircraft, there was an enormous
temptation to try to knock out the bases from which Skyhawks and Mirages would come. On the other hand, overt
as opposed to SAS-type attacks on the continent would have
provoked immense difficulties for the United States throughout the hemisphere. On 12 May, the Colombian Ambassador
told me that the first bomb to drop on the continent would
mean the automatic termination of diplomatic relations.
That a British Prime Minister should seriously contemplate
bombing mainland South America demonstrates how reckless
she had become.

The pinnacle of Mrs Thatcher's triumph may have come
on Saturday, 3 July, when she declared to a crowd of 5,000
of her supporters on Cheltenham Race Course that she
scorned the 'waverers and fainthearts' who doubted Britain's
ability at the outset of the Falklands campaign to 'do the
great things we once did'. The 'Falklands factor' was to be a
major new force in British politics. 'We have proved ourselves
to ourselves. It is a lesson we must not forget — the faltering
and self-doubt has given way to achievement and pride. We

have the confidence and we must use it.' We were still the nation that had 'built an empire and rules a quarter of the world'. Shades of Lord Palmerston in his hey-day of the 19th century! To no thinking person does this effusion of national will make any sense in the world of the late 20th century.

As a postscript, I ought to say that this view of the behaviour of the Prime Minister is not simply a matter of hindsight or being wise after the event. On Wednesday, 7 April, I warned the special meeting of the Parliamentary Labour Party in these terms: 'The farther South the Armada gets, the more impossible it will become for the Prime Minister to cry halt. How can Mrs Thatcher be in the position of the Grand Old Duke of York, who marched his men to the top of the hill and marched them down again, if the Argentinians don't—and they won't—pull out the troops from what they see as their Malvinas? Do you think this woman will stop it? Don't kid ourselves. Any efforts she makes towards peace will be a deception. She'll fight!'

15. What of the Future?

One of the most unsatisfactory aspects of the entire Falklands conflict has been the persistent refusal of the Prime Minister and her most senior colleagues to give any public indication that they have applied their minds to the long-term future of the Islands. They fact that they have advocated a range of possibilities, from settlement by substantial numbers of British people to the establishment of a permanent multi-national force, including the United States, suggests that their private views are no clearer than their public pronouncements.

Yet, from an early stage the Government were pressed as to their long-term thoughts, not only by those in Britain who dissented from the sending of the task force, but by the representatives of South American nations in London. In late April, Ambassador Roberto Campos of Brazil asked: 'What will you do, even supposing you gain military re-occupation of the Islands? The Argentinians will hate you; they are good saboteurs; they will get ever more lethal aircraft; they will give you a hell of a life!' And, as the Colombian Ambassador also made clear on his visit to the House of Commons on Wednesday, 12 May, if the option in South America lies between support for a continental power or an extra-continental power, most Latin American countries would opt to support the continental power, in a situation of conflict. On grounds of hemispheric solidarity, they would support Argentina.

Nor, in the long term, can Britain expect the same level of American support which we received throughout the actual conflict and epitomised by the crucial provision of Side-winder missiles, without which there would have been no military victory. Midway through June, the United States Government pleaded with Britain not to demand unconditional surrender. They feared the destabilising effect in Argentina and the turmoil which they believed would result from chauvinism. As the British spurned the wise counsels of the Americans, Washington felt no overriding obligation to help London, when it transpired that no Argentine rulers would talk in terms that were remotely acceptable to Mrs Thatcher. The American UN delegation made this clear at the time.

Moreover, just as Alexander Haig vetoed British bombing of
the Argentine bases on the mainland, so any American
Secretary of State will do the same in future. Washington will
never underwrite any arrangement that does not have the
long-term agreement of Argentina.

In years to come, when students begin to study the Falk-
lands issue in detail, one of the essential sources will be *The
Guardian* writings of Peter Jenkins and the editorials of Peter
Preston, the Editor. Never was the American feeling more
eloquently expressed than in the editorial by Peter Preston on
Saturday, 5 June, ten days before the cease-fire, when he
put these words into an imaginary American's mouth: 'You
British are scratching at a raw nerve right across the Continent.
And we—because we live in the continent—are taking all the
pain. This potentially could be the biggest crisis for Washington
since the Bay of Pigs. Your Mrs Thatcher goes on continually
about Marxist subversion: the President likes that. But she
may be handing the Soviets a monster bonus, unless this can
be settled—and that means settled . . . We're getting
exasperated because you British still don't know what you
want. You can't see beyond the end of your own noses. First
you insist that the Governor comes back, and the legislative
council (democratic or not) and full British Administration.
This is your cake of triumph. But then you want us—the
Americans—to row in and secure your triumph on the cheap,
by keeping our GIs on the islands, stooging around there in
perpetuity, to scare the Argentines off. You write the cheque—
we pay the bill: that is not on.'

Another factor which does not help the British Government's position is that President Reagan's administration
contains key men who are embarrassed by the whole
Falkland's conflict and may have something of a guilt
complex. I assert that President Reagan, in the autumn of
1981, authorised General Vernon Walters, the American
Ambassador at large, to discuss with the Argentine Government the possibility of a joint Argentine/American base on
the Falkland Islands in order to 'curb Russian penetration of
the South Atlantic' (Mrs Thatcher, in a letter to me, claims
that she knew nothing of these negotiations, and I believe her
on this point). During the discussions with the Argentinians,
General Walters gave it as his opinion that the British would

protest verbally but would do little else, if the Argentinians seized the Falklands. There is reason to believe that American defence strategists are still hankering after a South Atlantic Treaty Organisation, in which their main partners, for reasons of geography, would be the Argentinians, and which would look after American interests in the Antarctic. Certainly, Washington acquiesced in the Argentinian presence on the British island of South Thule, a gateway to the Antarctic, and knew that the 'scientists' were in reality Argentine naval personnel. What the American leadership is now looking for from Britain, in the way of understanding of the Argentinian position, is exactly what, now that blood has been spilled, Mrs Thatcher will find it difficult to concede. These same Americans have generally perceived what British Ministers have never wished to admit—the relevance of the Vietnam analogy.

On Thursday, 10 June, Defence Secretary John Nott came to the House of Commons and made a statement to explain why he could not tell the country the extent of the casualties which had been suffered as a result of the attacks on the *Sir Galahad* and *Sir Tristram*. During the exchanges which followed, I asked him, '. . . are we not slipping into a British Vietnam in the South Atlantic and before we go any further into the mire, should not the task force be withdrawn?' This caused Mr Nott to say, 'There has been a series of victories and some set-backs. With great respect to the hon. Gentleman, any analogy with Vietnam is entirely false.' The trouble is that the closeness of the analogy with Vietnam has not been sufficiently considered on the British side of the Atlantic. The American campaign was studded with victories. The capacity of American power to strike where and when it chose in Vietnam was unlimited, but at the end of the day, the objective facts were too strong. The Americans could burn the Vietnamese with napalm; they could defoliate their forests—but America could not overcome the facts of geography and the power of Vietnamese nationalism which grew with every blow America struck. That is the analogy with the Falklands. With American help, we had the power to repossess the Falklands. We deployed 25,000 men and 100 ships, 8,000 miles away. There we are and there we shall probably stay for at least a while. But, sooner or later, there

will be a declaration by more and more countries, following
the stance of Latin American nations, that they recognise
the Argentinian claims over these islands. Already Asian
countries, including India, have indicated to Latin American
countries that they are sympathetic to the cause of Argentinian
sovereignty in the Falklands/Malvinas. Encouraged by these
declarations, reminded of the sacrifice in blood on the *Belgrano*,
on land and in the air — the Argentinians will fight on, as any
people would, let alone those with a tradition of *macho*.
Sometimes the Argentinian forces will be little more than a
nuisance. But then, from time to time, fighting will flare up
into something larger, as their power to inflict blows on us
increases.

So, just as the Americans found themselves bogged down
in Vietnam and American public opinion grew to such an
extent that they had to withdraw their troops, so we British
in our turn will be forced to face the immense cost, possibly
in blood but certainly in resources, of the Falklands adventure.
Mrs Thatcher has bitten off more than the British can chew.
Supply by armed convoy for the foreseeable future; the ever-
present danger for the islands of sudden attack? It will be
more than a matter of 'token defence'.

One question that has never been satisfactorily answered
is why, when we are apparently prepared to offer such a
formidable commitment, we as a nation allowed ourselves to
act as we did for two decades and more? The truth is that
successive British governments were persuaded, on account
of the economic plight of the country, that it would be
impossible to maintain a force in the Falkland Islands that
would be adequate to repel an invasion and protect the rights
of 1,800 people. They therefore reached the conclusion that
the right thing was for sovereignty ultimately to pass to
Argentina, and that the best they could do for the islanders
was to negotiate on the basis of sincere conviction, to achieve
the best they could for them. The mission by Ted Rowlands,
when he was Minister of State at the Foreign Office in the
Labour Government of the late 1970s, no less than the
Nicholas Ridley mission originated in the hope that sovereignty
could be ceded in such a way as to satisfy the Falkland islanders. Even if that were not the case, no effective signal was
sent to Argentina in the run-up to the 1982 dispute that

there would be a military response on the scale of the task force. That, at least, Mrs Thatcher should have made clear to all concerned. Had it been clear to Argentina from all that was said and done by the Government in the lead-up to the invasion that they were always going to resist, even to the extent of killing hundreds, possibly thousands of people, those men in Buenos Aires who took the decision to go ahead might well not have done so. British governments encouraged the belief that Britain would hand over the Falklands, but did not have the guts to say so. The most damaging charge against the politicians of the last two decades is one of cowardice — of recoiling from the effects on British public opinion, from confronting the Falkland islanders with the naked truth — that Britain had neither the resources nor the will to guarantee them protection from Argentinian aspirations indefinitely and that they would have to get used to that disagreeable fact.

As the months and years pass, the events of the first half of 1982 will recede into history. Before going to the polls, Mrs Thatcher and her Government will try to make as much political capital as possible out of the military 'success' of the Falklands operation. The Prime Minister's claim on Cheltenham Race Course, that the Falklands had given Britain cause to abandon 'faltering and self-doubt', which had given place to 'pride and achievement', is doubtless a preview of many, many speeches to come. Ministers hope that in the future, and certainly by the time the Franks Enquiry (Falkland Islands Review Committee) has been able to report, the failure to forestall the invasion may come to be seen as irrelevant by the voters.

Alas, the problem of sovereignty over the Falklands will not go away. Sooner or later it will return, possibly out of a seemingly blue sky, to confound Mrs Thatcher or a successor. The danger inherent in the return of the problem in military form may well be obscured by concentration on the outcome of the Franks Enquiry and the enthusiasm of the British body politic for allocating blame on various possible culprits, ranging from the Prime Minister herself to Foreign Office officials for what occurred before 2 April. Who was right and who was wrong before 2 April will be a topic of endless and delicious speculation, which may obscure the mistakes made *after* 2 April and the mistakes still being made. On the other hand, at the time of the next military crisis, it may not be forgotten that pride was the mother of action in the despatch of the first task force, and that the spectre of politicians wrapping themselves in flags will no longer satisfy an increasingly sceptical British public opinion. With the Middle East in flames, following Israeli action against the PLO in Lebanon, it will be hard to argue that the British decision to confront aggression in the Falklands has made the world a safer place. As I have already said, Mr Begin publicly stated that he was only doing in Lebanon what Mrs Thatcher was doing in the Falklands. I believe, moreover, that the attack by the Israelis would not have taken place if American attention have not been diverted by the Falklands crisis.

Far from setting an example to other countries, the handling of the Falklands dispute may have enhanced the belief in war as a solution to international disputes. It is in the West's real interest to encourage Third World nations to resolve their disagreements by diplomacy and not by force. If aggression is to be shown not to pay, negotiation cannot be left sterile. Negotiations are more difficult after the spilling of blood than before. The accepted wisdom during the Falklands crisis that diplomacy and military pressure go hand in hand is a highly dubious proposition. They are in fact more likely to be mutually exclusive. Military pressure from the other side simply raised the hackles of both British and Argentinians.

Another even more disturbing factor in considering the future relates to the nuclear issue. One of the explanations that is being offered for Argentina's defeat in the Malvinas is the fact of superior British military technology, backed by the United States. There is a great deal of truth in the suggestion that, had it not been for America making available the Side-winder missile to the British Harriers, the outcome of the air battle over San Carlos Bay would have been totally different. But it was not only the presence of the Side-winder that is thought to have made a difference; had it not been for our nuclear-powered submarines, Admiral Inaya's Navy would have been able to do battle from home waters. Whether this would have made any real difference is not the central issue; what matters is the truth or myth that it was the presence of nuclear weaponry which contributed to Argentinian humiliation. (This, incidentally, infringed the Treaty of Tlatelolco, which bans nuclear weapons from the South American continent.) In early May 1982 the then Argentine Government gave the go-ahead to develop nuclear weapons. It had previously denied reports that it was doing so, but claimed that it had the capacity to build a nuclear bomb, if it made the political decision to do so. From my knowledge of informed opinion about Argentine industry through my links with *New Scientist*, I see no reason to doubt their claim to be able to produce a nuclear device 'within a year'. Given that the single most emotional event during the war for ordinary people in Buenos Aires was the torpedoing of the *Belgrano* by a nuclear-powered submarine, would it be easy to deny popular demand in Argentina for the possession of nuclear weapons? And once possessed, what response would we make to protect a British garrison in the Falklands? The implications are disturbing, to say the least, and should not be forgotten in any consideration of Britain's action in the Falklands.

16. Conclusion

By the middle of November 1982, we have seen the end of the beginning of the Falklands affair. At any rate for the time being, as we predicted, active armed hostilities have died down. But Argentina's diplomatic battle with Britain over the future of the Falklands/Malvinas is resuming. Predictably and predicted, Argentina is presenting, with the support of other Latin American countries, a draft resolution to the United Nationals General Assembly. The resolution will doubtless be the first of many calling for the resumption of direct negotiations to find a peaceful resolution to the dispute over sovereignty as soon as possible. It is likely that sooner rather than later Argentina will be able to muster a majority of the United Nations on her side. What then does Britain do? Mrs Thatcher will be characteristically dismissive of United Nations Resolutions which she does not fancy. She will make speeches about the sacrifice of British blood and the consequent impossibility of discussing sovereignty with Argentina. For her the impossibility may be real enough in terms of domestic politics: were she to talk to Buenos Aires in language which they would find acceptable, her leadership of the Conservative Party, threatened in early April 1982, would once again be at risk. People would naturally demand to know why all the sacrifice of blood and resources was necessary. Furthermore, remembering the response of Peter Shore and others in the opposition parties to the Ridley initiative, could she expect support from outside her party?

For Francis Pym, the Foreign Secretary, the diplomatic pressures from colleagues in other countries will become considerable. By nature, and by virtue of the fact that he was not party to the decision to sink the *Belgrano*, Pym would find it easier to carry out a u-turn. Any Foreign Secretary must become ever more anxious on the effect of a festering sore between Britain and Argentina on our trade. For example, Babcocks of Renfrew, makers of the biggest power station boilers in Europe, stated in September 1982 that they had lost multi-million pound orders in Venezuela and elsewhere in South America, 'at least partly for political

124

reasons'. Like Siemens, Aerospatiale, the Chase Manhattan
Bank and a host of other great enterprises, the firm which
won the power station orders, Mitsubishi, preserved their
relations with Argentina intact throughout the Falklands
crisis, whatever their Government spokesmen may have said
from time to time about supporting Britain.

Nor, in the face of critical UN resolutions will the position
of the Labour leadership be much more comfortable than
that of Mr Pym. Those who have nailed their Falklands
colours to the mast of UN resolutions can hardly forsake the
UN as it becomes critical of Britain. The sooner opposition
leaders get used to the fact that they are going to have to
support the concept of meaningful talks with Buenos Aires,
the better for all of us. Any hopes of a change of heart in
Buenos Aires, or that Argentinians, beset by economic and
social problems, will forget about the Malvinas, are wishful
thinking.

In Argentina the Government's general stretegy, since the
military set-back at Port Stanley, has been co-ordinated by
Senor Juan Aguirre Lanari, the Foreign Minister, who has
displayed considerable ability to muster domestic backing
among influential military and civilian figures. The approach
to the Falklands/Malvinas question has changed not one iota.
Senor Lanari in many ways represents the continuation of
the policies of Senor Nicanor Costa Mendez, Foreign Minister
in the Galtieri Government during the conflict. Certainly any
foreseeable Foreign Minister of Argentina would differ very
little in their approach to the issue, if at all.

The position in the autumn of 1982, at the start of phase
two of the Falklands affair, may be summarised as follows.
First, any Argentinian Government will refuse to sign a
formal cessation of hostilities with Britain. Second, Argentina
simply does not accept the British Government's definition
of the Falklands/Malvinas issue as a question of self-
determination; it holds that the matter is one of decolonisation.
Third, Argentina is turning increasingly to the non-aligned
movement for diplomatic support, though she also has hopes
of some help from the United States and certain European
countries. It has become clear beyond doubt that nothing of
the original problem of the Falklands/Malvinas has been
resolved by resort to arms. On the contrary, matters have

been conspicuously exacerbated by the spilling of blood. International disputes, at any rate between medium-sized powers, can only be settled by negotiation.

The refusal to contemplate signing a formal end to hostilities is based on a number of factors. It is consistent with the argument of the Argentinian armed forces that the surrender of General Mario Benjamin Menendez at Port Stanley on 14 June was a battle lost rather than the end of the war. Again, it is the almost religious belief of the Argentinian Foreign Ministry that formal cessation of hostilities would involve the recognition by Argentina of British rights over the islands. The lifting of financial sanctions between the two countries was a different matter, made necessary by Argentina's need to renegotiate her foreign debt.

However, it is not only Argentina that has landed up in a financial mess over the Falklands. The costs to banks in America and the City of London of the destabilisation of Argentina are unquantifiable. Britain has wildly underestimated the long-term costs, as I have indicated. On Sunday, 3 October, William Keegan, the economics editor of *The Observer*, wrote: 'There is going to be more reflation for the (1,700) Falklanders than for the entire (56 million) population of Britain in 1983/84, according to figures now circulating in Whitehall. Secret estimates for the capital costs of a new Falklands airfield, Phantom aircraft to be purchased from the United States, and an anti-aircraft system are now put at between £500 million and £1 billion, largely to be spent in the financial year, 1983/84 — about double earlier calculations. These figures are causing consternation in White-hall and among a number of Cabinet Ministers, at a time when the Treasury is asking for heavy custs in the departmental projections by the Departments of the Environment and Health and Social Security for the next financial year.' Small wonder that the imaginative Labour candidate for the Western Isles, Brian Wilson, should send a telegram to the Prime Minister, on the publication of the Shackleton Committee Report, advocating investment in the Falklands, to the effect that he would like Shackleton despatched to the Hebrides, along with similar resources to those proposed for the Falklands. As the memories of acts of individual heroism by servicemen fade from memory, so burning resentment at expenditure in the bottomless pit of the South Atlantic will grow among those who feel themselves personally under-paid, over-taxed or starved of resources for the publicly-financed projects nearest their heart. The words attributed to Abraham Lincoln, that 'You can fool all the people some of the time, and some of the people all the time, but you can not fool all the people all the time', are applicable to the Falklands affair.

The continuing financial commitment in the South Atlantic may not itself be the only or even the greatest cost of the Falklands war. To Protestant Ulster, the events of 1982 carried a message, perhaps a deceptive message, but still a message. Protestant Ulster does not now think it can be sold down the river. When the crunch comes, they argue, kith and kin will not be betrayed, whatever those 'scheming civil servants' in the Northern Ireland Office, the Cabinet Office and the Foreign Office get up to. Besides, to Protestant Ulster, the Falklands brought a bonus: icy relations between London and Dublin, on account of the Eire refusal to sever links with Argentina. The cost of the Falklands—in placing the possibility of compromise in Northern Ireland farther off than ever—may turn out to be very, very costly.

Moreover, the Falklands affair has highlighted the immense problems of dealing with what has come to be called the 'fag-end of Empire'. If a sudden crisis flares up in Gibraltar, or Hong-Kong, or Belize, are we to have the same hasty and costly decisions? What should the Opposition of the day do? In a sense, in such a situation the Opposition have a potential veto on Government policy. For it must be reiterated that it is inconceivable that even Mrs Thatcher could have despatched the battle-fleet to the South Atlantic, had not the action had the endorsement of the Opposition leadership. The task force could not have been despatched from an obviously divided country.

Last but not least, we must consider the question of British citizenship for all the Falkland islanders. It was a matter of heavy irony that on the afternoon of Friday, 9 July 1982, the Government Whips used their power of objection to block Robert Kilroy Silk's Bill to give 400 island-ers British citizenship. This action prompted the veteran columnist, James Cameron, to ask, 'What sort of a cheap lawyer's quibble is this? What was all that kith and kin Mrs

Thatcher was endlessly droning out in her Boadicea Act? Did those 255 British soldiers die 8,000 miles from home to protect the integrity of a community that she will not now acknowledge as countrymen?'

The background to the controversy is to be found in the 1981 British Nationality Act. One of the main aims of this legislation was to bring the law of nationality into line with immigration law. Citizenship as defined by the Nationality Act of 1948 no longer gave any clear indication of who had the right of entry into the UK. So three kinds of citizenship provided for in the 1981 Act define three different relationships with the UK. First there is British citizenship for people closely connected with the UK: generally speaking those whose parents or grandparents were born, adopted, naturalised or registered in the UK, and who therefore have the right of abode here. Second, there is citizenship of the British Dependent Territories for citizens of the United Kingdom and colonies who have that citizenship by reason of their own, or their parents' or grandparents' birth, naturalisation or registration in an existing dependency or associated state. The Falkland Islands are such a dependency. The third category is British Overseas Citizenship, for those citizens of the UK and colonies who do not acquire either of the other citizenships at the commencement of the Act.

Those Falkland islanders who do not acquire British citizenship by virtue of being patrial CUKSs, but are CUKCs with connections of birth or ancestry with the islands, will become British Dependent Territories' Citizens (BDTCs) when the Act comes into force on 1 January 1983. Of the 1,800 islanders, about 1,400 will be British citizens and the remaining 400 BDTCs only. As BDTCs they have no right of abode except in that dependency with which they have close connections. However, BDTCs who settle in the United Kingdom will be entitled to registration as British citizens after five years residence.

In the course of his speech on the second reading of the British Nationality Bill, the Home Secretary, William Whitelaw, said that special exceptions would be made for non-patrial Falkland islanders who wished to come to Britain. It may be, as he put it, that Falkland islanders would be given 'every sympathetic consideration', but, as Robert Kilroy Silk told the House, it is not sufficient to rely on the good will of the Home Secretary or the Government. If it is right to say that to all intents and purposes they have British citizenship, and that Falklanders will always be allowed to settle and work in Britain, then it is equally right to put that on a regular basis, and to enshrine it in law, by giving them British citizenship.

The reluctance to give 400 Falklanders full rights strikes a severe blow at the Prime Minister's good faith. For 70 days or more, Mrs Thatcher contended that we were fighting for a principle: to demonstrate that aggression does not pay, and that no country, be it a dictatorship or a democracy, can take over the territory and subjugate the citizens of another country. Mrs Thatcher also claimed that we were fighting for something more than that. She repeatedly said that we were fighting to protect *British citizens and the British way of life.* On her own criteria, therefore, should not the British way of life for which we sacrificed so much, apply to all 1,800 islanders, not just 1,400 who were fortunate enough to qualify for British citizenship? It is only one of many non sequiturs of the whole Falklands affair.

As the British novelist Salman Rushdie has said, Mrs Thatcher's 'are the politics of the Victorian nursery; if somebody pinches you, you take their trousers down and thrash them. The terrible, ironic effect of her policy has been that a war which we were told was fought to prove that aggression did not pay has ended up proving the exact opposite. The world's armies are already queueing up for Harrier jump-jets and Exocet missiles.' The best way in which Britain can do honour to the young lives that were lost and to our wounded and dreadfully maimed servicemen who will never be the same again — is to learn a lesson from the events of 1982 and make sure that such a situation is never repeated.

Appendices

APPENDIX A

A letter from the author to Lord Franks, Chairman of the Falkland Islands Review Committee (Franks Enquiry), dated 23 August 1982, submitting evidence for consideration, prior to his appearance before the Committee

Dear Lord Franks,

On 26th July 1982, you invited anyone who has information which might assist your Committee, in considering its remit, to submit evidence to you in writing by 30th August 1982.

My credentials for doing so are:

(a) Between 1974-76, and again 1979-80, I was Chairman of the Parliamentary Labour Party Foreign Affairs Group, and as such attended Foreign Office Seminars on, and interested myself in the Falkland Islanders' problems.

(b) In 1976, I was Leader of the British Inter-Parliamentary Union Delegation to Brazil, and subsequently have taken a special interest in relations between Britain and Latin America.

(c) As a member of the indirectly-elected European Parliament, I was one of the delegates chosen by the Socialist Group to represent them at the European-Latin American Conference in Mexico City in 1977, and took an active part in the Conference at Strasbourg when delegates from Latin America came to the European-Latin American Conference, which we hosted.

(d) Throughout the Falklands Crisis, I took such an active part in the House of Commons, that it was deemed to be incompatible with my position as Opposition Front Bench Spokesman in another area (Science).

I have little doubt that you and your colleagues on the Committee have been deluged with evidence, and on the grounds that busy men, working to a time-table, should be spared non-essential reading, I am putting my points in possibly over-succinct and staccato form.

Should you wish amplification, I would be happy to try to provide it. (I have completed a book, *One Man's Falklands . . .*, to be published by Cecil Woolf, probably in November, and should you, your Committee colleagues, or members of your staff, wish to see the relevant chapters, my publishers would be happy to make them available to you!)

Finally, should you and your Committee colleagues wish to hear any oral evidence from me, I would regard it as an absolute priority commitment to appear before you; though I would be grateful if Monday, 27th September could be avoided, as I'm committed to speaking at a large fringe meeting at the Labour Party Conference.

With good wishes,
Yours sincerely,

Tam Dalyell.

Legal Considerations

As you will have read, Lord Franks, in the House of Commons proceedings of July 1982, I urged the Prime Minister to appoint an international lawyer, like Elihu Lauterpacht, or Fred Parkinson, to your Committee and I maintain that it is a pity that she did not see fit to do so.

The claim, reiterated by Ministers, (for example, by Cecil Parkinson, on BBC 'Panorama') that the British claim to the Falklands was 'rock-solid' and that British Governments never had any doubts about it is palpable nonsense.

Ever since Gaston de Bernhardt, in 1910, a member of the Foreign Office Research Department, was asked by his superiors to do a paper, the Foreign Office have had deep doubts about the efficacy of the British claim – and have never had the confidence to take the matter to the International Court at the Hague. (Nor has Argentina taken it to Court: I am told that they have felt that European lawyers would tend to side with a European state: whether they were justified in such a view is another matter, that is what successive Governments in Buenos Aires believed.)

On 8 July 1982, Francis Pym, as Foreign Secretary, signed a letter to me, in the course of which he said, 'I do not think it right to concentrate on a few isolated and selective expressions of doubt.' The de Bernhardt Memorandum and what followed hardly constituted 'isolated and selective expressions of doubt' – on the contrary, these views were the result of required opinions, and central to Foreign Office thinking. Again, may I respectfully suggest to the Committee that your work would be incomplete, Lord Franks, without obtaining written and possibly oral evidence from current academics such as Dr Peter Beck, and Malcolm Dess, who have studied the work of Jules Goebel, the author of the authoritative work on the Falklands, published in 1927.

Is it not a fact that at various times, British Ambassadors to Buenos Aires, and senior members of the Latin American Department of the Foreign Office confessed having such doubts to Argentinian diplomats? I am not suggesting this was dishonourable: British diplomats may well have considered – rightly in my view – that good relations with Latin America were a more important British interest than the supposed interests of the Falkland Islanders in remaining under British sovereignty. I am suggesting that such confessions by British diplomats re-inforced the Argentinian view that Britain would not send a battle-fleet to wage war, against a country which had never been hitherto involved in more than a skirmish on the Paraguayan border. Your Committee, Lord Franks, is under an obligation to international opinion to reveal exactly what British Ambassadors and the Latin American Desk of the Foreign Office have been telling Argentine Governments over the last quarter of a century.

The First Warning of Possible Invasion to the Prime Minister

We have it on the authority of James Callaghan that each week – on a Friday evening? – a Prime Minister is given a special box, chiefly relating to advance warning of problems 'which could blow up in the Government's face'.

Bitterly resentful and seemingly aggrieved Foreign Office personnel, believing themselves to be much-maligned, have let it be known that neither they nor the Intelligence Service let Britain down. Doubtless they will be giving their own evidence; but some of us hold it as a matter of public concern that your Committee, Lord Franks, should give the British people the date on which the Prime Minister was first notified of the likelihood of invasion of the Falklands.

I believe that from early April, (after the period of your remit), Mrs Thatcher's whole demeanour was of a lady who positively wanted a fight, in the absence of Argentine humiliation, (and in my book, *One Man's Falklands* . . ., I show, in detail, step by step, how she scuppered the Peruvian Peace Plan).

Yet, confronted by the Prime Minister's denial, my American sources insist that 'the British Government' – maybe, not the Prime Minister herself – knew, as long ago as the end of 1981, about the idea of an American-Argentinian Falkland Base, and that for political hemispheric OAS reasons, any notion of an Anglo-American Falklands base was a non-starter.

Lord Franks, could your Committee try to ascertain who, and at what level, in the 'British Government' was told about the American negotiations in Buenos Aires, and whether the information was conveyed to Ministers?

There was a widespread belief in Buenos Aires that whatever crocodile tears might be shed in London publicly, privately ruling circles would be only too thankful to be rid of the difficult, intransigent Falkland Islanders, and that a military coup – not as shocking to South Americans as to Europeans – might be seen as a blessing in disguise. Furthermore, decision-makers in Buenos Aires imagined that they had a 'green light' from Washington for going ahead with an invasion. One question for your Committee is, 'Who in London knew of the American plans, and the Argentinian deductions from those plans, and by failing to say or do anything, tacitly encouraged the Argentine invasion?' For example, the Foreign Office must have known that the Galtieri regime was much more determined than any of its predecessors over the 'Malvinas', and that the Argentinian people set considerable store by getting the islands back, before the 150th anniversary of their 'take-over' in 1833.

There is one other possible scenario which your Committee, Lord Franks, will probably be examining. That the Prime Minister was indeed informed by her Foreign Office Ministers and senior Civil Servants of the likelihood of an Argentine invasion, and on the grounds that we did not have the resources to defend the islands, albeit reluctantly agreed to accept the *fait accompli* until on 2 April, Mrs Thatcher found herself confronted by the unanticipated fury of the press, feeding on the outrage of most Conservative and some Labour MPs. Realising that she was faced, not with a 'nine-day wonder', but with a substantial threat to her own political future, such a scenario would suggest that she reneged on indications of support she had given to her Foreign Office Ministers. In such circumstances, it would hardly be surprising if Lord Carrington felt himself to be double-crossed. But one hopes that the former Foreign Secretary's own evidence will clarify this aspect of the Falklands affair.

The issue for your Committee is, if I may say so, whether the Prime Minister was indeed given advance warning of an Argentinian invasion, and took a decision not to take preventive measures, in the expectation that the invasion would go ahead. Were this the case, it would not be a matter of 'crisis management', but 'crisis manipulation' for domestic political ends. In short, did the Prime Minister know what was likely to happen, and opt for being the nation of the 'injured party', so that she could lead the British people, in a fight which she thought that they would be likely to enthuse about, and which might take their minds off economic and employment problems? This attitude of 'let it run' is no different from that of Galtieri, who wanted to divert attention from the domestic problems of Argentina. I am conscious of the gravity of the charge that I am making against the Prime Minister.

But if the charge against the Prime Minister of wanting a conflict from a very early stage is ill-conceived, then one is forced to the conclusion, in the light of information now available about Argentinian planning of the invasion, and indeed of newspaper reports early in 1982 in Spanish language and American papers, that the Foreign Office/ Intelligence Services displayed mind-boggling incompetence. It is one or the other.

The Role of the Foreign Office

Ever since early April, the officials of the Foreign Office have been the subject of much virulent criticism from Enoch Powell, and many other MPs. Your Committee ought to be aware that a number of us in the House of Commons, with no axe to grind for the Foreign Office, or personal friends involved, have come to feel that the Diplomatic Service may have been much maligned over the Falklands; in particular, we have a distaste for the criticism of the Foreign Office by innuendo, in which some very senior Ministers indeed have indulged.

A good deal has been said about 'second-rate diplomats in South America' and to the effect that 'if Lord Carrington and Messrs Atkins and Luce had to resign, why not the officials who gave them the advice?' What advice? Bad advice which was accepted? Good advice which was rejected? Out of fairness to the diplomats concerned, your Committee ought to find out and tell the British public. Besides, what constitutes 'bad advice'? Supposing there was a value judgement by officials that the interests of 1,800 Falkland Islanders, as perceived by themselves, from their narrow vantage point, were outweighed, as far as the British national interest was concerned, by the sensitivities of 230 million Latin Americans, I would not label it 'bad advice'. Rather, I would see such a judgement as a realistic assessment of the world in the 1980s. Some of us recognise that numbers *do* matter. Furthermore, should your Committee decide that it has to criticise or censure certain officials, you would then in my view be morally obliged to clarify your views on the matter of resignation, if only because sections of the British public would be baying for the blood of the civil servants concerned. Suppose you put some official, sitting in a key advisory position, during the crisis, in the position of feeling compelled to resign. What good will it do? That official cannot, like a Minister, come down to the House of Commons, and make a statement to explain himself, speaking so eloquently that he makes the possibility of his early return to the Government front bench a certainty. Nor can that official explain himself or defend himself in writing. He is constrained by the Official Secrets Act, about which you, Lord Franks, know more probably, than any man alive. The official criticised is out, and for ever, and in silence. If criticism is going to be made of officials, some dispensation is going to have to be made to allow them to defend themselves.

There is one other matter relating to the Foreign Office, which I do not believe to be irrelevant to your Enquiry. This is the responsibility, fairly and squarely on the Prime Minister, of appointing a Foreign Secretary from the House of Lords, and not from the Commons. (As I argue as some length in *One Man's Falklands . . .*) it is inconceivable that a Conservative Foreign Secretary in the Commons would have had the battering from his own back-benchers, which they were prepared to hand out to a junior Foreign Office Minister like Nicholas Ridley. Had there been a more restrained Commons reaction, to what were the Ridley proposals, subsequent events would almost certainly have been different. For example, the Argentinians might have thought that the British Government was serious about an acceptable solution, and was not simply just procrastinating and prevaricating as they had done for 17 years. For all his contribution in South Africa and elsewhere, Britain has paid a terrible price for having a Foreign Secretary in the House of Lords.

The Role of General Vernon Walters

General Vernon Walters – distinguished ex-Marine Commando, ex-deputy chief of the CIA, negotiator in Vietnam, highly respected in the Republican Party, friend of the President of the United States, fluent Spanish speaker, Ambassador at large – was in Buenos Aires, intermittently, for many days, between October 1981 and February 1982. He discussed *inter alia* the setting up of a 'South Atlantic Treaty Organisation'. He also discussed the advantages for such an organisation of an island-base in the Falklands, somewhat along the lines of Diego Garcia. However, the understanding was that the Agreement on hemispheric and other grounds, should be between the United States and Argentina, the bulwark of American policy in the South Atlantic, and not between the United States and Britain. Asked by the Argentine military what Britain would do, the Americans replied to the effect that the British would 'huff, and puff, and protest, and do nothing', with the implication that the Americans could soothe the ruffled

British feathers. So much for fact.

Following my published letter to *The Times* on this subject, and a formal letter to the Prime Minister, asking for her comment, Mrs Thatcher denied knowledge of the activities of General Walters and his colleagues in Buenos Aires.

The Role of the House of Commons

In my respectful view, your Committee's Enquiry will not be complete unless you take a careful look at the activities of certain Members of the House of Commons over the last decade. In 20 years and more membership of the House of Commons, I cannot recall quite the kind of (partly seemingly orchestrated) mauling of Ministers from both sides of the House than Fred Mulley, during the time of the Labour Government, and latterly Nicholas Ridley had, as Foreign Office Ministers, attempting to put forward a sensible compromise solution to a difficult 'end of empire' problem. Bluntly, I think your Committee should look at the membership of/connection with the Falkland Islands Committee, amongst those who rose to be called by Mr Speaker, both during the Mulley and Ridley statements. I suspect that what emerged was a distortion of the view of the British House of Commons, as a whole, had it ever been asked to think about the future of the Falkland Islands, and more a reflection of the efforts of a well-organised lobby. All of us in Parliament have a heavy responsibility in the matter, in that we might have been expected to speak up; but the nature of our system is such that in consideration of 'recondite issues', it tends to be left to the few who have interested themselves: in this case, the 'few' tended to be cultivated by the Falkland Islands Committee. I am not suggesting that there was anything illegal in the activities of the Falkland Islands Committee, but rather that it ill behoves the House of Commons to ladle out criticism of the Foreign Office, and others, when we might do well to look at the 'mote in our own eye'.

The discreditable truth is that the House of Commons and successive Governments were not prepared to fork out the meagre £12 million for the Falklands, asked by the Shackleton Committee, nor were we prepared to have the guts to say to the British public and the Falkland Islanders that we were unwilling to finance economic help and military protection for them, and that they would have to come to arrangements with their Argentinian neighbours, who supplied not only fuel and victualling, but more and more of the health care and education necessary for any community. Our own collective House of Commons political cowardice contributed in great measure to the tragedy. It is hardly a mitigating circumstance that the majority of us in the House of Commons, engaged with other seemingly more pressing concerns, allowed ourselves to be wagged by a smallish tail of Members.

The Role of Two Particular MPs

Your Committee might care to ask the Rt Honourable Cecil Parkinson MP, (later as Chairman of the Conservative Party, to be a Member of the War Cabinet) and Neville Trotter MP, what exactly they did say to their Argentinian hosts on visits to Buenos Aires, and whether they are sure that they did not leave behind the impression that the Falkland Islands were expendable. As a Minister in the Department of Trade, Mr Parkinson was naturally concerned to promote the sale of British exports to Argentina. Mr Trotter is reported in *The Whitley Bay Express*, as having urged the Argentinian Government to buy warships, to be built on the Tyne, in the area of his constituency. I mention these cases, as it is wrong, in my opinion, to dwell simply on various 'green signals' to Argentina which may have been given by various British Ambassadors to Argentina at various times.

Indeed, I would not think it an absurd suggestion that your Committee ought to write formally to the present Argentine Government, Senor Costa Mendes and to newspapers such as *La Prensa* and *Clarin*, for their version of events before 2 April. There might be no reply; there might be an abusive reply; on the other hand, there might be a reply that helps your Committee to get at the truth of what did occur.

APPENDIX B

A letter to the author from Dr Peter J. Beck, Senior Lecturer in International History at Kingston Polytechnic, dated 28 May 1982

Dear Mr Dalyell.

Re The Falklands Dispute and Goebel's book

As a historian/international relations specialist who has been researching into the Falklands dispute for several years (in contrast to some of the instant history dished up in the media and parliament) I was interested to read in *The Times'* 'Diary' of your concern with the Goebel book as a means of examining the strength of British title to the Falklands. I think that this matter is of interest, especially as the Foreign Office have withdrawn 'for research' most of the files on the dispute's history since *circa* 1910; these files were at the Public Record Office, although even before the present crisis a large proportion of material on the sovereignty dispute was closed for 50-75 years (the Foreign Office comments on Goebel's book in 1927 are closed for 75 years).

The enclosed article was published in the USA in February, having been written in April 1981 when things were relatively quiet. However, as you can see from pp. 52-54 of the study, the Foreign Office has had doubts in the past about the strength of British title to the islands, doubts fuelled by the advice of legal advisers. The files cited in the footnotes for the quotes on title have all been withdrawn recently from the Public Record Office 'for research' by the FO. When the dispute broke in March/April I was on research in the USA, and hence unable to write very much as I was on a tight schedule. However, I was asked to write a brief item for *The Miami Herald* (enclosed), in which a range of aspects are covered (and the islanders and Parliament are blamed for their myopia and failure to appreciate the realities of the 1980s).

Upon my return I wrote a more specific study of the legal title matter, and criticising Pym's statement that we have no doubts and *never* have done about our claim (this is an inaccurate quote of a speech on 4 May in the Commons), a point repeated by Parkinson on 'Panorama'. *The Times* did not accept it (it was submitted at the time of the controversy over the media's coverage of the conflict), but *The Sunday Times* did. Their initial intention was to publish it in 'Insight' on 23 May, but apparently they opted out because of the above-mentioned controversy. Since then each Sunday has been dominated by military events (the study now belongs to them and is their copyright, and the study and my advice is being used in their projected book on the crisis). As a result, the British public has still not been presented with a balanced appreciation of the legal question. My study (which includes a reference to a 1946 FO memo closed in England but read by me overseas) indicates the uncertainty in the FO on Britain's title, especially after a FO memo written in 1910 on the history of the dispute (i.e. were the Falklands *terra nullius* or not?); these doubts persisted into the 1930s, encouraged by another historical memo of 1928 (this memo quoted Goebel as one of the sources), although by the late 1930s title by prescription was increasingly stressed, especially after the centenary celebrations of 1933. This offered a method of substituting a good title for a bad initial title. Nevertheless, this did not disguise the fact that some members of the FO believed that in 1833 Britain had acted like an 'international bandit', that is, no differently from Argentina on 2 April 1982. It appears that prescription and continuous effective preparation is the basis of the British case. However, in the past there were doubts. Goebel, while elaborating some points, did not add substantially to the legal situation (it was generally dismissed in the FO as an anti-imperialist polemic at heart for all its legal finesse – I have a 10-page appraisal of Goebel by the British embassy in Buenos Aires). The very detailed 1946 FO memo concluded that, in the light of the contradictory evidence on the claims for the pre-1800 period (e.g. a 1764 plaque preceded the British 1774 plaque, the uncertainty over the secret agreement) it was best to discuss the situation as from 1810-11, a matter upon which the evidence was far from clear.

I hope that these points are of interest, and, if necessary, I would be happy to respond to any questions that you might have (it is easiest to get me by phone at home . . .).

It might be of interest to ask a parliamentary question on historic doubts about British title deriving from the Bernhardt memo of 1910 and the other views quoted in my article in the light of Pym's statement and of the extended closure of most files on the subject.

Yours sincerely,

Peter J. Beck

PS. Have you any information on the events of 1968, when I understand that sovereignty was to be ceded. My information (which George Brown refuses to confirm – I wrote to him in January 1982) is that he decided to cede sovereignty but that Chalfont's weakness failed to convince the islanders. Also parliament took up the cause and forced a retreat. Is this correct? And was it Brown's initiative (I heard that he called a meeting at the FO and said that he wanted better relations with Argentina and had decided to cede the Falklands).

A letter from the author to the Foreign Secretary, Francis Pym, dated 22 June 1982

Dear Francis,

Three weeks ago I was contacted by Dr Peter Beck, a historian from Kingston Polytechnic who lives in Woking, the constituency of Cranley Onslow, to whom I am copying this letter.

In the course of his researches on the role of Antarctica in International Politics since 1890, Dr Beck has naturally studied the history of the Falkland Islands, both in Britain and overseas, as is well known to Dr John Heap of the Foreign Office.

You will have had brought to your attention the important article by Dr Beck on page 20 of *The Sunday Times* of 20 June. I would be interested in your comment on the following questions, arising out of Dr Beck's work:

(1) Whether or not Britain has ever offered to submit its claim to the Falklands to international arbitration?

(2) Where did you, and for that matter Mrs Thatcher and Lord Carrington, get the information, which formed the basis for your reiterated claim that there was no doubt about the British title to the Falkland Islands? This was epitomised, as I well remember, by Cecil Parkinson, on 'Panorama', opining that our claim was

'rock-solid'. This attitude contrasts with the statements by Dr Beck that: (a) in 1910, Gaston de Bernhardt, a member of the Library Department of Sir Edward Grey's Foreign Office provided a memorandum, which cast grave doubts on Britain's title, based on pre-1833 material; (b) either Richard Sperling or Gerald Sidney Spicer, the Assistant Secretaries, write, 'From a perusal of this memo, it is difficult to avoid the conclusion that the Argentinian Government's attitude is not altogether unjustified and that our action has been somewhat high-handed'; (c) Ronald Campbell (later Sir Ronald Campbell, Ambassador in Paris) concluded in 1911, that the best claim to the Falklands in 1833 was that of Buenos Aires; (d) the Gaston de Bernhardt memorandum provided the basis for the 1928 John Field memorandum, for which Goebel was used as a source, leading to doubts by Troutbeck and Fitzmaurice in the mid-1930s: 'The difficulty of the position is that our seizure of the Falkland Islands in 1833 was so arbitrary a procedure as judged by the ideology of the present day. It is therefore not easy to explain our possession without showing ourselves up as international bandits'; (e) the memo of 1946, by the Foreign Office Research Department, concludes our only real claim is through 'prescription', based on post-1833 criteria, and 'occupation'. One official, possibly Brian Roberts, in 1946, described our action in 1833, as probably one of 'unjustified aggression'.
(3) Could I have your view of the strength of the British title in international law, in view of *The Sunday Times'* statement (20 June 1982, p. 20) that the Law on Prescription is still relatively unchartered (*sic*), really 'uncharted', territory. Must this also not apply to the self-determination argument?
(4) Finally, I must ask you whether the Foreign Office doubt about British entitlement have influenced the Government's willingness to discuss the matter properly with Argentina?

Yours sincerely,

   Tam Dalyell

The Foreign Secretary's reply is dated 8 July 1982

Dear Tam,

Thank you for your letter of 22 June raising certain points on the history of the Falkland Islands. I have seen Dr Beck's article on page 20 of *The Sunday Times* of 20 June. On the four main questions you raise in your letter, I should like to give you the following comments:
(1) The British Government have never proposed that the question of sovereignty over the Falkland Islands should be referred to international arbitration. The situation regarding the Dependencies is different: see the enclosed *Hansard* extract [House of Commons, 27 April 1982, pp. 244-5].
(2) Successive governments of the United Kingdom have been advised that the legal title of the UK to the Falkland Islands is fundamentally sound and have always acted on that basis. You refer to a number of comments made in the past at various dates by individual officials in the FCO. I do not think it right to concentrate on a few isolated and selective expressions of doubt. The strength of our case depends on a detailed legal examination of all relevant events and factors. Even leaving aside arguments in our favour based on events before 1833, we have been consistently advised that our title can be soundly based on our possession of the Islands from 1833. Our case rests on the facts, on prescription and on the principle of self-determination. It is not affected by single comments taken out of context made by officials or even an Ambassador in Buenos Aires, especially when they were made many years ago at a time when our continuous possession

had lasted much less long and the principle of self-determination was not recognised as it is today.

(3) Prescription as a mode of acquiring territory is generally recognised in international law and is referred to in the standard works. It is certainly justifiable for us to rely on it in connection with the Falkland Islands. The current principle of self-determination is of more recent origin. But there is no reason why we should not refer to it in support of our legal arguments as a whole, since the population of the Falkland Islands have been established there for so long a period. It is widely regarded as relevant to decisions on legal rights.

(4) In all discussions with the Argentine Government the Government have of course taken into account the legal position and the legal advice which has been given to successive governments over the years.

Yours ever,
    Francis

APPENDIX C

A transcription of Brian Widlake's interview with John Silkin on BBC Radio's 'The World at One' programme, 2 April 1982

Brian Widlake: 'Well, after Mr Atkins' statement in the Commons, the Opposition Defence Spokesman, John Silkin, asked the Lord Privy Seal a number of questions, one of which was absolutely central to the crisis. Namely: had the Government misjudged the situation? I took this up with Mr Silkin and asked him whether he thought the Government had done exactly that.'
John Silkin: 'Well I do believe it has because I put the point that this tin-pot fascist junta that rules Argentina, whenever it really gets into trouble at home – and this one has – then starts foreign adventures. And therefore I think the signs were there that they were going to choose this as a pretext. And I do believe that had they . . . the Foreign Office and the British Government, taken notice of what was happening, we would have been in a much better state of preparation.'
Widlake: 'Do you think there's anything we can do about it at this stage?'
Silkin: 'Well, I think we have to defend our own people – because that's what they are – in the Falkland Islands. I think that their absolute desire, marvellous desire, to remain British has got to be respected; we've got to do everything we possibly can to help.'
Widlake: 'But the question is what are we going to defend them with?'
Silkin: 'Well, that is a question that I imagine is exercising the Secretary of State for Defence. We were warning him, we've been warning him from the Labour side for months now that what he was doing was neglecting our conventional forces in order to pursue his nuclear dream, which was costing far too much and forcing him to put surface vessels in mothballs or even not to go on with them. Now the result of that is that he may have given – I hope he hasn't – but he may have given the Argentinians the impression that we were prepared not to stand by our responsibilities in the area. That would be very wrong, we are prepared to do it and I think we're all united in that.'
Widlake: 'If we further assume that British naval vessels are on the way to the Falkland Islands, but (Yes) by the time they get there a landing would have taken place; would you go on to say that even though the landing had taken place, it was up to the British to get the Argentines off Falkland Island territory?'

Silkin: 'Yes, of course . . . I believe that's right and I believe it must be done. I mean effectively . . .'

Widlake: 'Even though there's fighting involved?'

Silkin: '. . . effectively that means a state of war has been created by another power, not by us. So it's British territory and it's British citizens, there's no doubt about that in international law. But of course there are other ways of stopping fighting or there ought to be. And at least the Government did in fact, go to the Secretary General of the United Nations and say "Look, this is a threat to peace and something must be done". So it is something to be said for them that in fact, the Security Council can be recalled if this sort of situation arises.'

Widlake: 'Well I wanted to raise this point with you because, as you know, you've just been saying that Mr Atkins said that if the situation worsens, Britain will go back to the Security Council. (Yes) But would that be likely to do any good?'

Silkin: 'Well, it can't do any harm. And at least I got from him a very important question I thought was, whether there was support for our point of view in the Security Council? And he said he thought there was. Now that can be helpful. But I do agree the important point is we've got to defend our own people.'

Widlake: 'And we must defend them in your view, even though it may mean fighting?'

Silkin: 'Certainly.'

Widlake: 'John Silkin, the Opposition Defence Spokesman.'

APPENDIX D

A transcription of part of BBC Television's 'Panorama' programme of 10 May 1982. The interviewer was Michael Cockerell

Cockerell: 'As the Task Force reached Ascension Island, half-way to the Falklands, some MPs began to express concern about its vulnerability to air attack. There was no doubting the power of the Navy's warships, concern was about air cover. In the Commons nearly a month ago, Tam Dalyell interrupted the Prime Minister's speech to ask about our assessment of the strength of the Argentine Air Force.'

(*recording*) Dalyell: 'Does she not know that there are at least 68 Skyhawks in the Argentinian Air Force, plus Mirages with R5-30s and this is a formidable force' (*interruption, several people speaking together*).

(*recording*) Thatcher: 'Mr Speaker, I have indicated to the Honourable Gentleman and to the House that we have taken steps to double the provision of the Harriers and we believe that will provide the air cover which the whole House . . .'

Cockerell: 'What concerned Dalyell was the military advice about the Falklands operation that the Prime Minister had received from the Chiefs of Staff in the Army, the Navy and the Air Force.'

Dalyell: 'Quite frankly, information came from a source that I've always found impeccable in the past, that some of the Chiefs of Staff, Air Staff, have not been happy and I looked Francis Pym and John Nott straight in the eye, they were both paying attention . . . every Member of Parliament has to take responsibility for his own statements. I am taking the responsibility of saying that some of the Chiefs of Staff advised against this whole mission to the Falkland Islands.'

Cockerell: 'Are you saying that the Chiefs of Staff, or the Chief of Air Staff, was unhappy from the first with sending the Task Force?'

Dalyell: 'From the beginning.'

Cockerell: 'They thought that it wouldn't be effective?'

Dalyell: 'They thought that there was great vulnerability.'
Cockerell: 'But you can't . . . you can't expect the Secretary of State for Defence to reveal publicly the advice from Chiefs of Staff to the Prime Minister on a mission like this.'
Dalyell: 'I assume that it would have been denied in the strongest terms.'

APPENDIX E

A letter from J. A. Gannon, Vice-President of the United Commercial Travellers' Association Section, Association of Scientific, Technical and Managerial Staffs, dated 7 April 1982, to the Leader of the Opposition

Dear Mr Foot,

I spoke with Tam Dalyell after today's meeting of the Association of Scientific, Technical and Managerial Staffs Parliamentary Committee, and told him that I agreed with his statement in the House on the occupation of the Falkland Islands by Argentina – that is, that the effect of British military action against Argentine forces would unite the 'Spanish-speaking world' in support of Argentina's claim to the Islands.
Having lived in South America, and knowing the feeling on this issue at first hand, I have no hesitation in saying that from Mexico to Punta Arenas the unanimous opinion would be that Argentina's claim to the Islands is a just one. The issue traverses across all ideological differences and, for once, there would be total agreement between the followers of Peron and Allende, Pinochet and Castro, Guevara and Galtieri.
Without, in any way, excusing the military occupation of the Islands by Argentina, it is my opinion that this question should have been resolved long ago by diplomacy in a way which will protect the interest of the Islanders and take account of the immense problem for the United Kingdom in seeking to perpetuate the status of the Islands at the other end of the Earth. I know that this is easy to state and difficult to achieve, but I hope that out of the present crisis will come a new and realistic opportunity to resolve the matter; in this, the islanders must recognise that what has happened in the past week could recur over and over again until an acceptable compromise is reached between Argentina, the United Kingdom and the Islanders.
The above is written at Tam's request, and I am sending him a copy; of course, it is all my personal opinion, based upon my own experience, and it does not purport to represent the position of others.

Yours fraternally,

John Gannon

A letter from the Argentine Refugees' Group, Joint Working Group, London N1, dated 21 April 1982, to the Leader of the Opposition

Dear Sir,

We are a group of Argentine refugees resident in the UK. We had to leave the country because we opposed the military dictatorship that took over in March 1976.
We are very concerned about the conflict in the South Atlantic.

This country has not only welcomed us, but also given us the opportunity to recover and re-start normal life. We have been able to study, work and enjoy the freedom of the UK.

The Argentine people have been claiming the sovereignty of the Malvinas/Falkland Islands for over 150 years.

We think that the issue over the Islands concerns Argentina as a whole and goes beyond political boundaries.

It is therefore untrue that the opposition to the military regime, even those who had relatives kidnapped or had to leave their loved ones behind, would like to see a British military victory over the Islands.

Unfortunately both countries are on the verge of a military confrontation, which would lead to a bloodshed of British and Argentine soldiers which every sensible and democratic person should be against.

We will be caught in a conflict between our native and adoptive countries, making the situation difficult for us in both countries, which we would regret deeply.

We ask you to end the attempt to retake the islands by force and accept the many offers of mediation offered by the UN or the OAS should Mr Haig's diplomacy fail.

We believe we speak not only for ourselves but for the great majority of the Argentine refugee community living in Britain.

Yours sincerely,
    Argentine Refugees' Group

Index